Money for Teens
A Guide for Life

Tim Wuebker

A Big Thank You

* To my parents, brother, and sister, all of whom shaped my values.

* To Dave Ramsey and Peter Adeney, who are wise advisors to millions each. Your inspiration was—and is—essential. Everyone needs both of you.

* To Nicole Kuhl for her kindness, wise professionalism, and witty creativity.

* To all of the incredible authors listed in **Part XIV: Reading, Viewing, and Online Quizzes.**

* To my generous and wise guest speakers, whose achievements, life experiences, and constant reading dazzle me: Bradie Armstrong, Ben Barrett, Matt Baysinger, Alex Bentzinger, Jacob Bentzinger, Tanner Bramlege, Andrew Brancato, Mario Brancato, Brian Bucklin, Kim Burnell, Jamie & Sean Cailteux, Anna Callahan, Ashley Carson, Michael Consiglio, Mike Debus, Bryan & Nancy Dorsey, Annelise Feder, James Ford, Matthew Fulks, Eduardo Godinez, Kenzie Grimm, Annelise Hammeke, Erin Hartegan, Jake Hellwig, Greg Hohensinner, Grant Huerter, Maddie Joerger, Ed Jones, Alli Jordan, Marcus Kain, Brenna Killen, Sammy Kopecky, Laura Lynn Lapoint, Jim Menown, John Muelhberger, Ferd Niemann, Lauren Niesen, Rob Oyler, Jesse Poole, Andrew Protzman, Micala Quinn, Dr. Shane Rapp, Jack Reilly, Larken Reilly, Blake Ripp, Dominic Rizzi, Larry Ryan, Cole Sheridan, Gina Smrt, Shannon Steer, Zac Storm, Allie Stuhlstaz, Tyler Supalla, Bianca Tropeano, Grace Vannoy, Lauren Vaughn, Joe Walberg, Mel Watson, Solveig Weinberg, Madeline Wohletz, Ashley Wurtenberger, & Megan Young. Any omissions are my responsibility.

* And to my many wonderful teens, whose energy and kindness always inspires me. Thank you for making my life so joyful!

CONTENTS

Part I: Core Essentials

1. The Least You Need to Practice

In this guide, I am doing my best to distill what I've absorbed from the millionaires I know, and from books by millionaires. From many conversations (and readings), I believe you will go far if you:

* Practice *excellent character*, which means having sky-high levels of honesty and integrity.

* Budget, keep a Balance Sheet, and do Dave Ramsey's 7 Baby Steps in order (or follow a similar plan).

* Open a Roth IRA or a Roth 401K *this week*, and invest *every year*.

* Think like a millionaire, and behave like one—not like a TV millionaire or like the middle class.

* Understand that your emotions will guide your behavior, and they will either make you rich or wreck your most of your plans, and not just your money plans.

* Ask God for help. When I had money problems fifteen years ago, I asked God for help. Since then, for 364/365 days out of every year, I have found free money. Sometimes, it's just a penny—just enough to remind me that God wants to help me, and that I need to make an effort.

2. God and money

God is more important than money, clearly. Your health and relationships are also more important than money.

That being said, sometimes people only quote the Bible once regarding money, when there are at least 72 powerful verses about money in the Bible. We shouldn't just take the lazy way out and misquote this verse:

"The love of money is a root of all evil." (1 Timothy 6:10)

Occasionally, people misquote this as, *"Money is the root of all evil."* That's too bad, because it makes some good people want to *avoid* money. But money can amplify a good person's good deeds.

Let's also quote, "The borrower is slave to the lender, and the rich rules over the poor." (Proverbs 22:7) The Bible also says, "One who lacks sense gives a pledge and puts up security in the presence of his neighbor." (Proverbs 17:18)

As you would expect, the Bible urges us to be honest, try to enjoy our work, and to be generous. The many verses on these topics should help us to develop our potential and to help others along.

It's too bad that these passages seldom get quoted because debt can enslave you. Do you want to work two jobs? Live hand to mouth? Not be able to quit a horrible job because your family needs the cash? Debt creates horrible situations, and it makes your life harder.

In life, who gets the money? If good people think money is evil and thus avoid it, doesn't that leave all of the money in the hands of bad people? What can gang members, drug lords, and crooked politicians do with lots of money, other than buy weapons and influence?

Any number of saints were wealthy. Saint Katherine Drexel was an heiress from Philidelphia, PA. Sir Thomas More was a lawyer. Blessed Pier Giogrio Frassati came from one of wealthiest families in Italy. Various royalty became saints, including St. Henry of France, and St. Elizabeth of Hungary. The list goes on. Of course, there are a lot of poor and middle class saints, too.

Money itself is merely a tool. Like all tools, it can be used for good or evil. I hope you become a millionaire and use the money 100% for God and to help educate the less fortunate.

3. Personal Finance is 80% Behavior and 20% Knowledge, and It's Hard to Say Which Is More Important

Dave Ramsey says personal finance is 80% Behavior and 20% Head Knowledge, and that's hard to dispute. Stephen R. Covey says every good action starts off as an idea. In other words, it all starts in your head—your ideas direct your life. But it better not end there.

The examples are endless. If you know how to save, invest, or budget money, but don't, then what good is *knowing* how to save money? Isn't that like knowing it's expensive and unhealthy to smoke a pack of cigarettes per day, but you're not going to do anything about it?

So, *this guide is not here to motivate you.* I hope you're already motivated, and willing to take action, because I believe that when good people get rich, they do inspirational things: they save a starving child's life! They fund a good cause! They create jobs so that others can work and feed their families! Just by being productive, they help society advance, which should lead to the cures of diseases!

Instead, this guide is meant to be a fast reference, where you can quickly go to the section you need, learn something essential, and then put it into action.

And throughout, I point you toward many astonishingly compelling and enlightening authors.

Many books on personal finance are 500 pages long. Some of them are outstanding, but my goal is to concentrate on the essentials and help you get the nuggets you need as soon as possible.

And that's why this book is so short.

Part II: Practical Advice

4. The 7 Baby Steps

Most people *don't have a plan* that makes sense for their whole lives, but people who use Dave Ramsey's 7 Baby Steps do. Here they are:

1. Save $1,000 in an Emergency Fund

2. Pay off all debts using the Debt Snowball

    a) List all debts from smallest to largest. Ignore interest rates (unless one of your debts is to the IRS, someone dangerous like the Mafia, and/or if this an extremely special case).

    b) Make minimum payments on each debt.

    c) Except for the smallest debt! Throw everything you have at that. When that debt is gone, throw everything you have at the *next* smallest debt.

    d) Repeat until your debt is gone. From now on, always stay debt-free.

3. Increase your Emergency Fund to 3 to 6 months' salary.

    3a. Now we relax just a little and enjoy life. We save for whatever we want to buy.

    3b. Pay for a car, or skip this step.

    3c. Pay for college, or skip this step.

    3d. Save to put down 10 to 20% on a house, or rent and skip this step.

4. Pay off your house early. (Always take out a 0-15 year fixed-rate mortgage.)

5. Save for your kids' college.

6. Save 15% toward retirement.

[Steps 4, 5, and 6 happen simultaneously, and are interchangeable.]

7. Save, invest, and give in extraordinary amounts. Do everything with money that you've ever wanted to do.

If you don't like these steps, then you should re-think them and write your own version. You need a plan. Most people don't have a plan, and the average credit card debt in America is over $8,000. Many people have nothing in savings. Plan almost always beats no plan.

Important note: I believe everyone needs Dave Ramsey!

While there are many excellent personal finance books, podcasts, and shows you could read or listen to, Dave Ramsey's incredible common sense, kindness, and spirit of constant learning makes him indispensable. Thus, I urge you to read his book, *The Total Money Makeover*. While I'm not enthusiastic about asking you to spend money, *The Total Money Makeover* would be great for you to buy: new or used. Then you can read it nine times. I did.

4b. Do You Know What's Even Better Than the 7 Baby Steps and Budgeting? F.I.R.E.

Financial Independence Retire Early, or *F.I.R.E.,* is a movement popularized by Mr. Peter Adeney, whose popular blog is at mrmoneymustache.com. The basic premise? You can retire in your mid-thirties if you just do three things:

a) Save 70% of your income.

b) Invest exclusively in index funds. These are the mutual funds that have the lowest fees possible and yet, since they've existed, basically mirror the stock market. That means, on average, they return 9.5%. That beats about 99% of everything else out there.

c) They don't live in Los Angeles, New York, or any other city with a horrid cost of living. There are thousands of wonderful cities in America and other countries, so they live there.

I recommend that you do the "My Friend Will Have $1,000,000 by Age 35" that's in the exercise. He's a twenty-something teacher at my school who saves about $3,000 per month. As far as I know, he invests heavily in Vanguard index funds like I do. I invest in these ones:

VFINX: Vanguard 500 Index Fund Investor Shares. It captures the entire S&P 500. As of this writing, since March 6, 2009, it is up from about $63 per share to $270. It has an expense ratio of .14, which means they charge .14% per year to manage your funds. In an industry where 2 to 6% can happen, .14% is basically zero. And yet very few mutual funds have outperformed VFINX.

I am also in:

VDAIX, which went from about $12.50 to $46 in the decade from March 6, 2009 to June 2019.

VTSMX, which went from about $18 to $72 in that same decade.

I tell you what I invest in for two reasons:

1) Financial advisors who don't disclosure their investments drive me

crazy. How do I know if they're any good?

2) You can look these funds up yourself simply by typing their five letters into any search engine. All kinds of graphs and reports will show up.

You deserve to be able to do your own research. Ultimately, what you do with your money is your responsibility. My responsibility is to teach you everything I know so that you can make informed decisions.

5. The Three Quickest Ways to Have More Money: Income, Expenses, and Selling Stuff

For most people who'd like more money, these are the three most obvious areas to work on:

a) Raising income (see **Part III: Start Your Own Business Now** & **Part V: J.O.B.s, Careers, and Personal Missions**);

b) Cutting Expenses (see the rest of **Part II: Practical Advice**); and

c) Selling Stuff.

To sell stuff, read #59 *Space: Your Physical Environment and Your Stuff*, and #61, *Annoying Things*. Not only will you make money, you'll also make your place beautiful, which will help make you happy. And *Happy People Make More Money* (see #66).

6. Monthly Budget

I urge you to make a simple, one page budget first, and only use complicated budgeting software as an afterthought, if at all. Many millionaires:

a) Do their budget on one sheet of paper.

b) Or they carry around cash, perhaps stuffed in envelopes.

c) Or they use a simple budgeting app on their phone. (There are dozens, maybe hundreds.)

Like athletes who eat the exact same thing every day in order to simplify their lives, or pilots who use checklists to fly airplanes (which have literally 1,000,000 parts and are the most complicated machines on earth), millionaires use *simple systems* that a fourth grader can understand and use in 30 seconds so that they'll stick with their plan.

You should do a budget because:

* It's your money, so tell it where to go or it will disappear all on its own.

* You'll probably never wonder again where you spent that $20; you'll always know.

* 72% of all Americans *don't* do a budget--and they're in debt. The average credit card debt is over $8,000. Annual interest on that: $1,440. How many hours per week is that at your work? (#6i, *Opportunity Cost*).

6a. What a Budget Looks Like

There are many examples online. Personally, I keep it simple; mine is only one sheet of paper long.

Page One Contains:

* List of Income Sources, with amounts

* List of Expenses, with amounts

* List of things to sell

Page Two Has:

    * A list of the Active Expenses, and under each of which there is room to subtract as you spend.

If you don't want to use a paper budget, I recommend that you:

Use the envelope system.

Or download an app.

Finally, please do the "Budget Case Study" in the **Appendix.** It goes beyond Income and Expenses, and will help you with six wonderful concepts that will help you save money and be happier—and Happy People Make More Money *(Chapter #66).*

6b. Categories Your Budget Absolutely Needs, Like Entertainment – No Exceptions

Most people's budgets have about 6 to 30 categories. Absolutely you'll need:

Savings.

Debt Elimination?

Groceries.

Fuel.

Insurance.

Phone?

Entertainment. People think entertainment is a waste if money is tight, but if you try to be perfect all the time, I'll bet you $500 you'll stop budgeting and then really waste all your savings.

Far-off events, like *Christmas* or *Clothes Shopping*.

Charity!!! Most millionaires are givers. J.D. Rockefeller, the richest man in human history, tithed when he was in his early twenties and in debt. He tithed his whole life, and he and his son always gave away millions. I apologize for this example if you dislike J.D. Rockefeller, but the more you read actual books (and not articles) about him, the more you find that he was a kind person—and he succeeded in teaching his whole family to be givers (See **Part X: Millionaires Think Differently Than the Middle Class**, and read books by Dave Ramsey and his mentor, Dr. Thomas Stanley. They don't write about Rockefeller, but they explain how thousands of millionaires behave.)

6c. Get an Instant Raise

Most people who consistently budget find that anywhere from $100 to $500 starts to show up every single month.
They *plan it out.*

Ask people who carry written budgets around if this is true: "When you started budgeting, was it like getting an instant raise? How much?"

6d. Get a Raise Next Year

Most people find it hard to *save right now*, but they save just fine *in the future.*

So do this: tell yourself that the next time you get a raise, you will *tithe 10% of it and save the entire other 90% of it.*

In other words, let's say that next summer, you get a raise of $100 per month. Charity gets $10 and $90 goes into savings, and you keep living as you are—all the while knowing you're doing so much better for yourself. You just saved your entire raise!

6e. Quit Your Horrible J.O.B. That's Killing You

Let's say you have six months' worth of expenses in the bank as an Emergency Fund. You used to love your job, but you just got a new boss. What if he's not a nice guy? What if he's dishonest? What if you now hate your job? What if you're going crazy?

Most of the time, people say, "Don't quit your job until you have something else lined up." People also say, "Don't be weak; toughen up."

Almost always, that's good advice—especially when the economy has high unemployment—but in my observation of people, there's one major exception: when your sanity/health is at stake.

What if you're not able to make a great contribution because the system is backward?

What if they frustrate you?

What if you're becoming a negative person?

What if your stress is making you develop a dozen bad habits: over-eating, over-spending, and the like?

The first thing you must decide is: is it me or is it them?

If it truly is them, and not you: **quit**. You can do this if you have no debt and an Emergency Fund. That's why we budget in the first place.

If you have a lot of debt, you'd probably better have a new job lined up before you leave. Otherwise, you're screwing yourself over.

6f. Don't Work for Free

Without a budget, most Americans spend every dollar they make. After an entire month's worth of work, they are no better off.

How are they not working for free?

What's the point of their job? Especially if their job is a J.O.B.? (see #29, *Get a Job*).

6g. My Spending Is Out of Control

I think most people think this is a *logical* problem. Just spend less, right? Wrong. While it's possible that someone doesn't know how to make a simple one-page budget, it's more likely that they have an emotional block.

See:

+ 6h. *Increase Your Fun While Paying Less*

+ 6j. *Is Your Problem Logical, Emotional, and/or Environmental?*

+ Part XI: The Rest of Your Life Will Either Make You Rich or Make You Angry

+ Part XII: Family, Friends, and Spoiled Brats

6h. Increase Your Fun While Paying Less

Every time you do a monthly budget, also do "Fun vs. Happiness." Often, we spend

money in a weak effort to *have fun* or *buy someone else's friendship*—and we find out it doesn't work. We have very little fun, we feel like we've wasted our time, and the other person doesn't like us any more than when we started. Money can't buy you love (#76, *Dating*).

The "Fun vs. Happiness" guides are in the **Appendix**. Here's a preview:

Do This for Every Category in Your Budget

1. Make three columns on a blank sheet of paper:

a) ACTIVITY YOU'VE DONE or ITEM YOU BOUGHT IN AN EFFORT TO HAVE FUN.

b) WHAT WERE YOU REALLY TRYING TO ACHIEVE?

c) HOW COULD YOU HAVE GOTTEN THE SAME THING EITHER CHEAPER OR FOR FREE?

2. List twelve activities or items you buy under the first column.

3. Complete the second and third column.

Examples

#1: High-Priced Food

a) ACTIVITY YOU'VE DONE: Dining out with friends.

b) WHAT WERE YOU REALLY TRYING TO ACHIEVE? Have fun with friends.

c) CHEAPER OR FOR FREE ALTERNATIVE? Eat before going out; order one V8; just hang with friends.

#2: Expensive Movie

a) ACTIVITY YOU'VE DONE: See new movie for $8 to $15.

b) WHAT WERE YOU REALLY TRYING TO ACHIEVE? Entertainment with friends.

c) CHEAPER OR FOR FREE ALTERNATIVE? Check out free movie from library and have a house party. Added benefit: now you're Party Planner! You don't waste money, and your social life gets a boost!

6i. Opportunity Cost

Whenever you don't see the point of budgeting, consider *opportunity cost.*

Opportunity cost is a term economists use to point out that you can't spend the same $100 twice. That is, if you spend $100 on entertainment, that's $100 you can't spend on something else.

If you already put something in the budget—like junk food, or fun with friends—that may be fine. If you've planned it, if it makes sense in the larger context of your budget, go for it! Have fun!

But just like you have limited time, you have limited dollars. When you spend either time or money, they are gone.

6j. Is Your Problem Logical, Emotional, and/or Environmental?

From the book *Switch: How to Make a Change When Change Is Hard,* by Dan & Chip Heath, comes the concept that when people or organizations have a hard time changing, their problems are either:

* Logical (they don't know how to do something);

* Emotional (they aren't motivated enough); or

* Environmental (their home, school, or work is filled with obstacles).

When changes are hard to make, the true obstacles might be hidden. Logic often says, "Try harder!" But sometimes, your true problem is emotional, or environmental, or a combination of all three.

For example, let's say Chad & Macy are trying to save money. But:

* Maybe no one ever showed them how to budget. (Logical: they don't know how.)

* Their parents always give them money whenever they ask. (Emotional: why bother saving if there's always someone else's money to

spend?)

* Everyone around them spends freely all the time. (Environmental: It's hard to be the lone ranger.)

Switch: How to Make a Change When Change Is Hard was one of the greatest books I ever read, and it changed how I understand people. For more information and several handy one-page guides, check out heathbrothers.com.

7. Debt Is Stupid. At Least, That's What the Bible Says

* The Bible never says, "Don't borrow money." It just says you're a slave if you do. Consider these quotes:

"The rich rules over the poor, and the borrower is slave to the lender." -- *Proverbs 22:7*

"It's stupid to guarantee someone else's loan." -- *Proverbs 17:18*

If it's stupid to guarantee someone else's loan, how can it be *smart* to borrow?

Exception: it's probably okay to borrow money when you're *trading assets*—but a lot of conditions have to be met.

For example, let's say you borrow $200,000 to buy a house that's worth $200,000. You are trading the cash (asset) for the house (other asset).

Of course, there are many reasons it might be bad to do this. You may have to pay a high interest rate. Maybe you can't afford the payments. Maybe you'll lose your job next year and still owe $190,000 on the house.

At least, with trading assets, if you get fired and your financial life collapses, you can always *trade the assets back*. You can sell the house and erase the debt: no harm, no foul.

I've touched on some of the problems with houses, but there are more. See #18, *Renter, Owner, and/or Landlord?*

Borrowing is *sold* to us as a great idea, but you should read **Part IV: Pay for College without Loans** and **Part III: Start Your Own Business Now)**.

Finally, a lot of debt is simply credit card debt, which probably went for food and entertainment. In any case, whatever they bought is probably gone now and there's nothing to show for it (except maybe an item that's gone down 90% in value).

8. Debt Trips Up Your Opportunities

Cora Caitlyn, 23, has no debt. Ryan, 29, owes $155,000 on his student loan, and has credit cards. (I changed Cora Caitlyn's and Ryan's names.)

Cora Caitlyn

* Dean of students at a junior high school.

* Head counselor at a local children's hospital.

* R.A. in college.

* Volunteer leader of Reservoir, a Catholic event every month attended by 60-70 people.

* Paid for her own college.

* College graduate.

* Pays own rent.

* On time with everything.

* On top her finances.

* Returns every call.

* Working on a graduate degree.

* Open to advice; takes it.

* Saves every gift dollar from grandma.

* Pretty relaxed about money, even though she's worked all the time since age 15.

Ryan

* Part-time jobs at two clinics.

* Nowhere near his dream of running a clinic.

* Makes pointless sacrifices for others that usually involve advancing his credit card, like buying them dinner.

* Volunteers frequently. Can step up and lead.

* Owes $155,000, not counting other debts.

* 5+ years of college, but no college degree.

* Did get his advanced degree, so he is Dr. Ryan

* Lives with three men in a three-bedroom house; they have one floor.

* Runs late.

* Lost heat one winter because he ignored the Final Warning from the energy company.

* Many people say he's impossible to get ahold of.

* Doesn't know what he wants to do with his life. Has turned down job help.

* Looks brave; does not take advice.

* Late with bills even when he has the money; forgets to pay them; gets fined.

* Emotionally stressed out of his mind.

I asked Cora Caitlyn why she *always gets promoted*, and soon becomes the leader. She said, "Because I do everything that I say I'm going to do."

Both are fun people, excellent Christians, adventuresome, open-minded, and a joy to be around. They are great friends, and I love them.

And I love you, which is why I'm being so honest about Ryan's struggles, above.

Both are a lot of fun—but who would you hire?

9. You Need a Big Reason to Avoid/Eliminate Debt, or You Just Won't Care Enough

I can't motivate you. I assume you're already motivated. (#3, *Personal Finance is 80% Behavior and 20% Knowledge, and It's Hard to Say Which Is More Important*).

We've all heard stories of 100-pound Moms ripping the doors off of burning cars to save their babies. When you care enough, you can do incredible things fast. Examples:

* You will do everything your coach says if you really want to play.

* You'll study for ten hours to keep that A in your most challenging class.

But if you don't have a Big Reason, you'll hit snooze, surf the Internet, and waste time.

Q. Do you have a Big Reason? Have you clarified #31 & #32, your *Personal Mission?*

Practice *Generosity*, *Gratitude*, and *Character* (#68, 69, & 70). Pray to be happy, because *Happy People Make More Money* (#66).

10. Your Balance Sheet

A *Balance Sheet* is simply a list of all of your assets (and what each is worth) and all of your liabilities. It lets you know how much money you have. You need this to see where you are, financially. Example:

$6,500	Savings
$2,500	Checking
$1,000	Money Market
$2,000	IRA Money Market
$5,000	IRA Index Fund
$17,000	**Total Assets**

Liabilities

$5   Parents

$5   Total Liabilities

Net Worth = Assets – Liabilities. In this case, net worth = $16,995.

You can include things you own like cars, electronics, and clothing, but you could also say, "What's the point of including items that only go downhill in value?" Soon, they go to zero. Listing them under assets will only fool you into thinking you're richer than you are.

Once, I had a car with 262,000 miles that was 13 years old. I would have been shocked if it were worth $500 to anyone else, but a new one might cost me $15,000 to $25,000, so what was the car worth to me? Should I list it at $15,000? I didn't list it until it died at 284,500. It saved me money, but I didn't list it as an asset.

The only material item I would list as an asset is a house. That can be sold. But even houses as assets have complications (#18, *Renter, Owner, and/or Landlord?*)

11. Cars: Think Like a Millionaire

How Do Millionaires Buy Cars?

According to *The Millionaire Next Door*, by Thomas Stanley, most *future* millionaires buy used cars that are 12-18 months old. They buy the car outright, with no payments. According to Dr. Stanley, millionaires know exactly how much value a new car loses—in just the first week! (Up to 25% of its value.)

Later, when they actually have $1,000,000 in cash, then if they feel like getting a new car—even though it's not the best deal—they get one. A $40,000 car is nothing in their world. But at that point, many of them just don't care about having anything that fancy anymore.

Millionaires Use These Two Methods

1) They find a dealer they trust, tell him what they want, and let him go to work. This is slightly more expensive than the second method, but millionaires don't have to spend any time shopping around this way, and they have peace of mind that they are getting a great car because they use the same dealer repeatedly.

2) Or millionaires do a ton of their own research. They read *Consumer Reports*. They make comparison/contrast tables. Then they shop around, negotiate, and get the best deal. This is more work, but if you like doing this kind of thing, then you are behaving like a millionaire.

Do These Things

* Millionaires ask, "How much is the car?" People who are stuck in the middle class say, "How much is the monthly payment?" Think like a millionaire.

* Do not borrow or make payments; you'll pay an extra $2,000 to $7,000 in interest.

* Use the Five Keys to Negotiation (**Part VIII**).

* Ask what cars last the longest and need the fewest repairs. Try Hondas, Toyotas, and Ford Focuses, for example.

* Cars that are 12-18 months old cost somewhere between 50 to 75% of the brand new version. That's a massive discount.

* Remember that cars lose 10-25% of their value within one week of purchase.

* Accept that a car is a hunk of metal that is dying the minute you buy it. Millionaires know this. The middle class can get caught up in cars as a status symbol. (See **Part X: Millionaires Think Differently Than the Middle Class**).

* Every dollar you spend on a car might be a dollar that could have saved you from a terrible job, funded your college, or gone into your investments (and made you millions). See *#6i, Opportunity Cost.* Two examples:

* $20,000 invested in an index fund that grows at 10% will be worth $1,280,000 in 40 years.

* $20,000 spent on a car will be worth $50-500 in eight years.

A great method if you don't have much money to get a car worth any amount you like:

1. The average car payment is almost $500 per month. So, save $400 per month for 10 months.

2. Buy a $4,500 car with your $4,000 by paying for it in cash. (You might be able to do this if you negotiate. See **Part VIII: The Five Keys to Negotiation**.)

3. Over the next ten months, save another $4,000. Take that $4,000 + your $4,500 car and use those to get a car worth $8,000 to $10,000.

4. Do it again if you like to get a car worth $12,000 to $15,000.

Skip the Not-Completely-Honest Car People and the Hidden Headaches

Payments contain a lot of hidden trickery.

My friends who sell cars for a living point out that when you finance, *you tend to get outsmarted.* The lender at the car dealership processes loans 40 hours per week all year long. They know all the tricks.

You, however, might buy a car once every eight years. So, when it comes to loans, the lender is like a *calculus teacher* and the average person is like a *grade school student.*

They over-complicate these loans, and offer many complex options *for their benefit.*

I am sure many are honest, but even the honest lenders hope you will finance the car, because you could pay many $1,000s extra in interest. Then there are *late penalties, hidden clauses, extra expenses, and more hidden stink bombs you'd never sign up for if they were crystal clear about all the burdens.*

You can *eliminate* every hidden cost and complication by *not getting a loan.*

They also *prey on your emotions* when you choose payments. It's so much easier to go with every creature comfort and new optional technology and/or gadget. I have a friend who once got a sunroof because the dealer said, "It's only an extra $20 per month." With a five-year loan, that's actually an extra $1,200—not counting interest on the $1,200, which came to another $1,200.

These financiers basically understand their customers better than the customers understand themselves. They know the numbers baffle us. They know we're going to get emotional and lazy and want all the nice features. Even if they're honest, they're experts at this game, and we're beginners. So don't play the game.

Signing up for payments equals getting ripped off.

12. Electronics

The awesome thing about electronics is that they go down in price. Flat screen TVs were once over $3,000; amazon lists them for $300, now. So don't buy the latest version; get the previous. The new iPhone can be $600. The previous might be $150. You can probably even be thriftier than that.

* Don't upgrade so much.

* Consider buying used.

If electronics are your favorite thing, then budget for them, and don't feel bad about it. (#6a to 6j.)

Just make sure that you own them, and they don't own you.

13. Clothes

* See *The Best Way to Shop*, in the **Appendix**, but I'll summarize it for clothes here:

1. Inventory *all* of your clothes.

2. Use various methods like SPACE and *The Life Changing Magic of Tidying Up* to get rid of everything that doesn't give you joy.

3. Given that now you know exactly what's in your new (smaller) wardrobe, make a list of everything you need.

4. Find the most cute and fashionable women you know who *have no debt* and *don't necessarily make much money* and go shopping with them. They will help you look great and functional.

Once, I went with two friends who always look fantastic, but we spent about $500 too much. Too late, I realized that while they *didn't make much money*, neither one of them had ever had a job, and they both had massive credit card debts. Oops.

That's when I figured out: I need to buy clothes with women who are: cute, fashionable, and *debt free*.

The larger point is: shop with debt-free experts! (#35, *But Who Can You Go to for Advice When You're #1?*)

But I Hate Used Clothes

Then buy them for other people as gifts.

My Mom found an amazing black coat for $3 for me, and another winter coat for $26. I thought she spent $100-$250 on each. Far from feeling ripped off, I was thrilled that she found such great items for me *and spent so little*.

14. Furniture

Advice.

* Buy used. Used furniture can go for $5 to $100.

* New furniture can easily be $1,560 to $3,000.

* If you bought a $2,000 couch today and sold it next week, you'd be lucky if you got $100 to $250 for it.

* Furniture is *hard to sell.*

* Is furniture a *scam?*

So why don't more people buy used?

Q. How do you know they don't? Can you always tell used from new?

Q. They probably haven't thought of it. If all of their neighbors are buying new, it may never have occurred to them.

15. I Want New Stuff, Not Used Stuff

Go for it!! But only *if*:

* It fits into the larger context of your budget

* You've taken the steps in "The Best Way to Shop" (see the *Appendix*).

I have a friend who saves up. She always has the best of everything: the finest clothes, furniture, cars, and house. You could say she's highly materialistic—not like a hoarder (#60), but more like the most elegant of persons. She waited three years to buy an 18th Century French wrought iron table. Personally, I am not like that, but she is amazing.

You could also say she is highly patient because she has no debt.

I believe 100% that you should get the item you truly want, and not a substitute. You'll never wear or use the substitute, you won't like it, and even if it was $1, that makes it a waste of time and money.

16. Insurance

* Insurance is boring--*on purpose.*

* And frustrating.

* They talk in jargon.

* They try to manipulate us by exploiting our fears.

Perhaps they make it so boring because they know most of us only look at it once a year (or less), and they'd prefer that we just pay them a lot, even though we are unclear about what we're getting.

* Thus, people frequently get ripped off. They pay a lot for very little.

If you understand this, then this advice will make a lot more sense:

Advice

* Insure the *big things* (like houses & cars) and skip the little things (like electronics).

* Visit the agent in person before buying so you can *look them in the eye.*

* Stand up so you don't fall asleep.

* Take notes.

* Ask catastrophic questions like, "What happens if I hit a tree while driving? What do I get from the insurance company?"

* Write your questions the day before, and revise them.

* Don't buy anything on the day you visit. Take the information home and think about it.

* Once you do buy insurance, mark your calendar for a year from now, when you will review all the insurance you have, and see if it's still the

right kind. People pay insurance companies on autopilot. This is an expensive mistake. For example, maybe you should get expensive coverage for a newer car. But for an eight-year-old car?! Get the cheapest kind.

The best advice?

Insure the big things and skip the little things. Self-insure for the little things. That is, have an emergency fund.

Dave Ramsey has a lesson on insurance in Financial Peace University. It is excellent, and about the clearest and engaging presentation on earth of this monumentally boring topic. But you must understand: *it's boring on purpose.* Whoever stays awake keeps all the money.

17. Credit Cards

If you owe $1,000, you could pay $180 in interest on that every year.

My friend owes $15,000 on his card. That's $2,700 in interest every year. He's in hot water, and—despite his high salary—there is really no way he's ever going to pay that off on his own.

Typically, if a credit card company gets you to revolve $800 every month, you will be in debt for the rest of your life.

People say you "need to build your credit score." Not so. You can do this by paying your electricity bill every month.

People build credit so they can borrow money. But the only money you may ever need to borrow for is a house. (See *#7, Debt Is Stupid*.).

Q. Would you rather have $5,000 in the bank, no debt, and a nonexistent credit score, or would you rather owe $5,000, have no savings, and have a perfect credit score?

I'll take the $5,000 in the bank, no debt, and nonexistent credit score. Who cares what the credit score people think?

18. Renter, Owner, and/or Landlord?

You must decide for yourself between #1, #2, and #3, but these are listed in my order of preference:

1. Be the owner and landlord: Buy a house and rent enough rooms to friends so as to cover 100% or more of your monthly payment.
2. Buy a house with a 15-year fixed rate mortgage.

3. Rent with friends for $300-$500 per month.

4. Buy a house with a 30-year fixed rate mortgage. Yes, you'll pay 125% more interest than option #1, but at least you're building equity, and you can do anything you like to your own property.

5. Rent a one-bedroom apartment for $600 to $800 per month.

* See *Renter, Owner, and/or Landlord?* in the **Appendix**.

18b. Your House Is Not a Moneymaking Asset

This gets a little complicated, and owning a house mostly beats renting—by a wide margin!—but many people really don't understand that your house will not make you any money.

A house *is* an asset in the sense that if you own a $200,000 house, maybe you can sell it for $200,000, minus about $12,000 in fees and taxes. (Or worse.) So, maybe your $200,000 house *can* get you $188,000 (or less).

But if we say *an asset is something that puts money in your pocket* and *a liability is something that takes money out of your pocket,* then most houses are liabilities. I hope yours is a *doodad,* which is *something that's stranded between an asset and a liability.*

Why doesn't a house put money in your pocket? After all, doesn't everyone *say* a house is an asset?

I read a personal story in the *Wall Street Journal* from a couple who bought their house in New Jersey for $166,000 and sold it twenty years later for $500,000. So, it tripled in value! They made $334,000! That's a *third of a million dollars! That couple is rich! Their hard work paid off!* Right?

"Before you congratulate me," the husband wrote, he specified what they paid in taxes, insurance, interest, and repairs. "And we did *very few repairs,*" he said. Final cost: $498,500.

So, over 20 years, the couple made $500,000 - $498,500, which is $1,500, or $75 per year. That's a doodad.

Scenario

Your parents have 16 years to go on their mortgage—and the U.S. economy plunges into recession, and they both lose their jobs today.

Yesterday, they may have said, "Our house is an asset." But today, unemployed, they have to ask, *Do we have enough money to pay the mortgage? And for how many months?*

If you can't pay the mortgage, your house will not feel like an asset.

Remember

 * Owning houses beats renting. If you paid $500 per month in rent for 20 years, you'd have spent $120,000 and have *nothing to show for it*. At least the *Wall Street Journal* couple made $1,500. *And* they have a house.

 * When you rent, you have so few freedoms. Can't paint, can't garden, sometimes can't have pets, can't modify the property. You're cramped, restricted.

 * The lease you sign is terrible for you, too. Once, I read a friend's lease all the way through. It listed 25 things that put all of the blame and responsibility on the renter. The owner only had to do 1 thing. This is normal for contracts: people who write contract tend to slant it 99-100% in their favor. Have you ever read your employment contract? If you didn't write it, it will list 10-50 things you'll be penalized for, and it will list about 3 points like salary and benefits that are in your favor.

 * The best options involve paying for the house outright or within 15 years. If you work *Rent vs. Own* in the **Appendix,** you'll see that the exact same $100,000 loan will cost an extra $50,000 if you get a 30-year loan—and you're tied up with debt until you're much older. And being tied up with *Debt Trips Up Your Opportunities* (#8).

Part III: Start Your Own Business Now

19. Make $2,000 Using the Skills You Already Have

What do you love? Sports? Music? School? Working outdoors? Working indoors?

Q. Can you:

+ Tutor a school subject, like math, physics, chemistry, Spanish, or English?

+ Give sports lessons, like tennis, golf, baseball, or basketball?

+ Teach piano, guitar, or voice?

+ Clean people's houses or offices?

+ Take photos or create videos?

+ Create websites?

+ Do yard work?

+ What do you like to do?

Q. Can you advertise on social media? Can you tell all your friends? Can you talk to people in your neighborhood?

Q. Can you sell a subscription for your services for 6 to 12 months?

People who can tutor, for example, can set themselves up at *universitytutor.com* and charge as much as $25 to $47 an hour. If you do a good job with one client, sometimes word of mouth can create so much business for you that you won't have time to do it all, and you'll have to hire your friends to help you.

Congratulations, you're now a small business owner! You will become a:

+ Self-starter;

+ Champion of time management;

+ Rapid learner;

+ Smarter risk-taker;

+ Decisive person;

+ Clarifier of your own goals and preferences;

+ Thrilling person because your passion will shine through;

+ Terrifically generous person!

Is there any doubt that you will learn a lot and have something of an adventure?

20. Borrowing to Start Increases Your Chance of Failure

Maybe I'll ruffle a few feathers here, but every statistic I've seen indicates:

* You can start your own business for free. Chris Guillebeau wrote *The $100 Startup*, in which every person in the book made a minimum of $50,000 per year and started for somewhere between free and $600. The average person: $374. Guillebeau actually found 1,500 people who fit that description.

* Most of the businesses that fail start with borrowing—well over 60%.

Why do businesses that borrow often fail?

* Borrowing indicates laziness. Instead of solving your own problems, and learning as you go, and enlisting friends to help, people think they can simply buy success. This is like buying a gym membership—and never using it. People *think they're doing something* when they buy the gym membership. But they're not.

* Similarly, borrowing indicates an inability to think through free/cheaper alternatives. *(See 6h. Increase Your Fun While Paying Less.)*

#8. *Debt Trips Up Your Opportunities*. Why not *Make $2,000 Using the Skills and Passions You Already Have* (#19). And find friends and family members who will help? Have you thought through your *Personal Mission* (#31 & #32)?

21. There Are Only Four Ways to Make Money, (and Being a Business Owner Is a Great One)

* Employee → Risky.

* Self-Employed → Risky.

* Business Owner → Risky.

* Investor → Risky.

Make $2,000 Using the Skills and Passions You Already Have (#19) and you're "Self-Employed," or a "Business Owner." More on this later (*#31, The Four Ways to Make Money*), and in *#41, Risk vs. Reward.*

Nothing in life is ever certain. Even great employees get laid off in a shrinking economy. Ask ten adults around you if their job is 100% guaranteed—and see if you really believe them. Ask them three questions that start with the words, "But what if...."

That's why you need an Emergency Fund. (See #4, *The 7 Baby Steps.*)

Part IV: Pay for College without Loans

22. Pay for College in Advance; Don't Get Loans

1. Apply for 20 to 1,000 scholarships. Use the *Ultimate Scholarship Book: Billions of Dollars in Scholarships, Grants, and Prizes* to find scholarships; this 770+ page book lists about 4,000 to 5,000 scholarships. Writing 14 per day for 75 days during the summer = 1,050 scholarships. If you received 3% of these, you'd have 30 scholarships.

2. Or, like my friend Cora Caitlyn, pick your shots *very carefully*. Cora Caitlyn applied for *five* scholarships and received *four* of them. And while she's smart, she wasn't a National Merit Scholar or a person with 800 SATs.

3. Look where no one else is looking, because those scholarships go unclaimed.

a) Keep your eyes open for things (& scholarships) that no one is advertising. Local organizations give scholarships, and don't necessarily post anything online. So don't just look online.

b) Use the *Ultimate Scholarship Book: Billions of Dollars in Scholarships, Grants, and Prizes*. Online searches might just lead you to the same places that everyone else goes.

4. ***Do the essay scholarships!*** Many people don't like writing essays, even about themselves. If only two people do an essay scholarship, your odds are great. You can always get a friend to help.

Two *billion* dollars in scholarships goes *unclaimed* every year. Take advantage of this.

5. Simply ask the college for scholarships. Cora Caitlyn let Benedictine know that she loved their school and wanted to go there, but needed another $1,000. They made her an R.A., which gave her leadership experience that probably helped her score two leadership jobs within a year after she graduated.

6. Work one, two, or many jobs. For two weeks while transitioning, Cora Caitlyn worked *three*.

7. Save every gift dollar.

8. Go to community college for the first two years. Q. What's the difference between Composition I at community college vs. a prestigious private school. A. Most likely: nothing.

9. After community college, if you must borrow to attend a prestigious private school, then go to ESU (Enormous State University) instead.

10. Always remember that the quality of your education depends upon the quality of your instructors—*but it depends even more on the quality of your efforts, what you read, and how you spend your time!* That's why many people get a better education at a community college or an ESU than others do at a prestigious private school. What good is the world's greatest professor if the student doesn't meet him or her halfway?

11. *Prestigious* is easily the most overrated category of life on earth. If you were running a business, would you hire someone who can get the job done, or just someone who went to the "right" school?

12. *Don't Be a Statistic* (#23).

13. What's your *Personal Mission* (#31 and 32)? Know why you are going in the first place; maybe you'll graduate in 3.5 to 4 years. About 53% of the people who start college *will never finish it.*

14. College is a supplement to your education; read three books and you're an expert (#35, *But Who Can You Go to for Advice When You're #1?*)

15. Emphasize financial education and work ethic just as much as academic education (**Part X: Millionaires Think Differently Than the Middle Class**).

. 16. Double major, or at least seriously map out how this would play out over college if you did it.

17. One major must be practical and lead to a moneymaking skill. If my friend said, "I'm majoring in theatre!" (Or philosophy, psychology, English, etc.) I'd say, "That's awesome. I support that 100%. *What's your other*

major? And do you love it, too?"

18. You must *love both majors,* or when the going gets tough, you'll abandon the one you chose just for the money.

19. The person who chooses a career solely for the money will never make much money (#66, *Happy People Make More Money*).

20. Concentrate on the fundamentals of the school, not the sales pitch. Every college has the core classes that you need to graduate, so don't borrow $40,000 for a fancy college when you can get the exact same thing at community college & ESU.

21. Put just as much time thinking about your life from age 22-26 as you do thinking about 18-22. Do you want to work 60-80 hours a week to pay back student loans? Or would you like to be free?

College is four or five years out of your life. People forget that they are going to live until 80, so they get hung up on what they want to do right now. Parents hate to tell their kids no, but at age 18, you're an adult, and you're the person who experiences #8, *Debt Trips Up Your Opportunities.*

23. Don't Be a Statistic

1. 53% of the people who start college in the U.S. *never graduate.*

2. 25% of all freshmen (also called first year students) *flunk out.*

3. 40% of all sophomores and juniors drop out.

4. 73% of all students now take five years to graduate.

5. In 2011, 50% of all college graduates could not find employment. That was after the Crash of 2008. Even so, you can't just think having a diploma is all you need.

6. People get student loans that take 15 to even 30 years to pay off. But college is supposed to be an investment. What kind of investment puts you in debt?!

7. According to a meta-study done in 2011 and recorded in the book *Academically Adrift,* 44% of all students after their first two years have demonstrated *no real learning.* After four years, 36% have demonstrated no real learning.

8. Employers often are testing to see what students know before they hire because they've learned the hard way that many college graduates are "credentialed" but not educated. That is, they have a pointless piece of paper—a diploma—that doesn't necessarily represent anything.

Having taught eleven kinds of college courses for twenty years, I am convinced that the #1 trait that college graduates have in common is: they know why they are there (#31 & 32, *Personal Mission*).

When you don't know why you are in college, classes often seem abstract, pointless, and not fascinating. It is hard to go to class, read the books, and do the assignments when you aren't sure why you're doing any of it. People will go into burning cars to rescue a baby because they are intensely motivated, but they'll hit snooze six times if they have nothing really great to look forward to. Learn your Personal Mission (PM) and then only go to college if college fits your PM. At UMKC, hundreds of my students were non-traditionals (between the ages of 25 and 60). Frequently, they made the best students. They started off behind but usually finished near the top because they were crystal clear on their goals.

24. As a College Student, Think Like a Millionaire

Millionaires look at *underlying value,* not surfaces (**Part X: Millionaires Think Differently Than the Middle Class**.) So while often there's nothing wrong with going to a prestigious and expensive college, if the *underlying value* of the first two years is essentially the same at a community college or ESU compared to a $35,000 per year school, millionaires might easily choose the cheaper school.

It depends on what they're getting in return.

Millionaires also look at Return on Investment (ROI). Taking out loans creates a *negative return.* You *lose money.* What kind of investment puts you in debt?!

Some people are taking *fifteen to thirty years* to pay off their student loans.

If people were only in debt for three months after college, I could see the point. I wouldn't like it but I could see it. Even though 99% of everyone who has crippling debt probably started off with *just a tiny loan.* Just like most chain smokers probably only started off smoking one cigarette. At first, most people think this is just a tiny loan—I won't be like the average American with $8,000+ in credit card debt, a student loan, car loan, and a 30-year mortgage. With all of those obligations, you'll never *Quit Your Horrible J.O.B. That's Killing You* (#6e).

Millionaires are crystal clear on what they're actually buying. **College has, at most, three purposes.** They are to help you:

1. Acquire an *outstanding* education and have a life of the mind.

2. Get into a good job or career, and to live out your *Personal Mission* (#31 & 32)

3. Socialize and meet like-minded people.

Surely a *motivated* student can do all three *almost anywhere.*

Caution

A few of my degrees were in English, so when you tell college admissions counselors or department chairs that you want a good *return on your investment* and *you don't want debt*, often they will change the subject and talk about the glories of their campus and/or how college is a golden time in your life where you can read great books, think noble thoughts, and have a life of the mind, like a scientist, author, or philosopher.

I love great books, thinking noble thoughts, and having a life of the mind, but that's **Purpose #1,** *above.* Get them back to talking about **Purpose #2**, which involves getting a *financial* Return on your Investment. As such, college should *make* you money, not be a case where *Debt Trips Up Your Opportunities* (#8).

People who truly love great books will become life-long readers. And information is often free.

Part V: J.O.B.s, Careers,

and Personal Missions

25. Get Hired: Job Interviews

1. Apply in Person; Certainly Not Just Online

While it may be necessary to fill out an application online, it hardly ever gets anyone a job. When the economy crashed, any number of businesses might literally receive 3,000 people submitting their resumes online. No one reads them. The business might have software choose a few resumes on the basis of search words.

For as long as I can remember, at least 70% of all jobs are had by people who already know who you are. In the age of the Internet, that's more true than ever. Employers are like everyone else: they want to feel like they are making intelligent decisions based on having a lot of information. Like everyone else, employers *like the people they already know.*

But what if you don't know anyone? Then you must *create a connection.*

There are many ways to do this. I've sent in a letter of application *and then followed it up by calling them, and arranging a visit.* I've seen others get their friends to introduce them to the manager. All of these methods work. You can send a letter (or email) first and then follow it up within a week with an in-person contact.

With this method, you can even apply for positions that aren't open. That's how I was hired at UMKC, Rockhurst University, and Olathe North High School. Seven of my friends did the same within the last few years, getting anything from entry level work to $122,000 per year.

After you go in for an interview, the managers will tell you that they are sorry that they don't have anything available. But then two weeks later, after someone quits, you're the first person they think of, and they feel like they already know you.

If you don't already have a connection, that's one way to create one.

2. Every Employer Ultimately Wants to Know Just Three Things

They want to know about your:

+ Character

    * Honesty.

    * Reliability.

+ Personality

    * You work & play well with others.

    * You fit the profession. People don't expect accountants to be gigantic

        extroverts, for example.

+ Skills

    * Experience.

    * Education.

    * Transferrable Skills.

Sometimes, Transferrable Skills are the best category. For example, this is when someone who coaches one sport switches to a completely different sport—or perhaps becomes a leader at work. If you've done something *like* the job you want, then you have transferrable skills. They can ask you, "Have you ever led a team at Sprint?" You can reply, "I have leadership skills because I…"

When you have Transferrable Skills—and you do!--you don't necessarily need "Education" or "Experience."

3. Every Question Answers the Exact Same Question

Understand that no matter what they ask you, what they are really asking—in disguise!—is, "What can you do for us?"

If they ask, "What sports do you like?" for example, even if they're just trying to be social, subconsciously, they are still trying to get a sense of how well you work with others, how ambitious you are, what makes you passionate, or what you can do.

You can always re-direct your answers back to the hidden question. For example:

"What sports do you like?"

"I love basketball. Basketball is all about teamwork and the need to have a playbook. And when things aren't working, you have to be willing to create a Plan B. I learned so much about life from being on a hard working team."

On some level, here's what the interviewer hears: *Teamwork...playbook/planner...Plan B/flexible...learner...hard worker.*

4. Never Complain, Unless You Have a Solution in Mind

Sometimes, in interviews, they like to ask "negative questions," which sound like an opportunity to complain. For example, "Tell us about the last time you made a very thoughtful decision, weighed the evidence carefully, and it turned out that you were wrong." Or, "What did you like least about your last job?"

It's a trick question! Don't fall for it!

Primarily, they want you to be *honest*—and positive. So, tell the interviewer--*in one sentence, not two*--the honest truth, and then say *how you solved the problem.*

They want to see if you are a problem-solver, and a non-complainer, or if you have any number of negative traits (like complaining, gossiping, and/or laziness). We all have negative traits and negative moments. But they want to see your problem-solving side.

5. Exceptions to These Rules

* If you don't need the job, you can be as honest and direct (and even as negative) as you like. They may want to hire you even more because you're such a truth-teller. In a world of political correctness and social niceties, people who are simultaneously good-hearted and yet utterly real are refreshing. Good-hearted truth-tellers are always truthful, and they'll always do their best.

* If you get the sense that your interviewer has *no tolerance whatsoever* for the polite tones in which many people express themselves, and he or she always "keeps it real," then be an unvarnished straight-shooter yourself—very honest, direct, and potentially undiplomatic. Honesty needs to go both ways.

6. Finally, Remember That You Are Also Interviewing Them

In our society, it's easy to forget that every job interview is a two-way street. We focus so hard on pleasing the interviewer that we can forget to ask them some excellent questions in return.

What if you don't like the manager? What if they want you to work long hours for dirt wages? What if the potential coworkers are nasty people? That's why you need an Emergency Fund (#4, *The Baby Steps*) so you can *Quit Your Horrible J.O.B. That's Killing You* (6e).

In almost all job interviews, they will ask, "Do have any questions?" At this point, you should *retrieve a sheet of notes where you've already written out several questions.* If they give you terrible answers, then your experience with them will only go downhill from there.

26. Be Aware That Hiring Processes in America Are Messed Up

Surveys consistently indicate that somewhere between 50-60% of all Americans are unhappy in their work.

Other surveys indicate that employers consistently feel like they made a lot of hiring mistakes—perhaps as much as 50%.

Putting two and two together, I'd say that if half of all employees don't like their jobs, and half of all employers feel like they keep making wrong decisions, then our hiring processes in America are messed up.

Certain companies, like Zappos, are deeply aware that most hiring is poorly done, so they have a highly original process. Great companies will never say, "Well, that's just the way things are." They know that thriving employees work harder and are on fire. That's better for everyone. So, they don't hire the way most people hire.

In your life, eventually you will probably help out with hiring. I strongly recommend you study the best practices of companies like Zappos.

You must be counter-cultural. The unhappy workers make a lot of noise to the point where they make it seem like everyone is unhappy. But many people love their work. They love to help others and they feel satisfaction and accomplishment.

Once per month, review your *Personal Mission* (#31 and 32). Are you living your true life?

27. Seven Jobs Everyone Should Have for Six Months or Longer

Your character is your destiny. I honestly believe we'd live in a ten-times better world if everyone had these seven jobs for six months or longer—even if they did them every day for their parents, for no pay.

a) Clean up after others.

b) Meet the public.

c) Manual labor, like construction, field work, or cleaning things.

d) Leadership. For example, take kids to work or the park; and the kids need to come home productive &/or happy.

e) Care for an animal (and help it thrive and be happy).

f) Care for a plant.

g) Money management. For example, perhaps budgeting an event for others.

It's terrible when people think they are "above" certain kinds of work. The opposite of most of these jobs is being a *Spoiled Brat* (#79).
I've known poor people and rich people who think they're smarter, better, or above. Elitism is unattractive, to say the least. Snobbery has nothing to do with money.

Plus, when you become wealthy, it is good to remember where you came from. It will make you happy that you don't have to clean toilets anymore, and *Happy People Make More Money* (#66). Sometimes, you see people who are *Wealthy and Unhappy* (#65). You can avoid this.

First generation millionaires work hard. These seven jobs will shape your identity, and help you truly experience that **Millionaires Think Differently Than the Middle Class (Part X).**

28. Get Promoted and/or Get a Raise

Just as often as not, the best workers in the world *do not get promoted.*

Think about it: if you are doing an A+ job in your current position, the organization is thriving, and everyone is happy—why would anyone give you a raise or a promotion? After all, they think you're perfect right where you are.

To get a promotion:

Be as Effective as Possible

* Use the 80/20 Principle and *do less work*, but do that 20% even better than before. (The 80/20 Principle is outlined in the **Appendix**, in *The Best Way to Shop*)

* Keep up with the changes in your profession.

* Treat everyone from the leader to the custodian like gold. There are no little people. Everyone matters.

* Work all day long; don't take more than a five-minute break every hour.

* Cheer people up.

* Always be honest and have the highest integrity.

Promote Yourself

The best promotion is probably to be generous toward others. (#33, *Givers, Matchers, and Takers: Who Makes the Most Money, and Whose Careers Go the Farthest?*)

Because no one likes a shameless self-promoter, some people work very hard and hope someone will notice. But sometimes, no one ever notices. So unfair!

But many leaders and managers spend their entire month handling crises. They are overworked themselves. They don't necessarily step back and think about how excellent you are, and often, they spend zero time helping you develop your talents.

So, you must take control of your reputation, career, and direction in life and sometimes—and then let them know what you've been up to.

Diplomatically, of course. Usually after being a Giver (#33) yourself.

Most of All, You Must Learn and Do Your Manager's Job

Getting back to the idea that if you do your job perfectly, then they may be scared to move you, *you must demonstrate that you can do the job that you want to move into.*

Otherwise, you have what they call "on the job training." That's fine in lower level positions, but think about how easy it is to promote someone to a new position where they've already *demonstrated that they can do the work,* and that they *have a desire to learn more.* Who would you make into a head coach? The faithful lower-level coach—or a coach with an undefeated record from some other school? Often, promotions go to people who have already demonstrated that they have the necessary skills.

So, do your best to master the position you'd like to move into.

Help other people solve their problems—without enabling them (#79, *Spoiled Brats*).

Be generous.

In Fact, Think Like Your Manager, and/or Like the Owner

Do you know what many managers see every day? Various employees running to them with problems that the employee asks the manager to solve.

So, when they see certain employees coming, they think, "Here comes another headache."

The best career advice I ever received was: solve your own problems first, and don't tell anyone there was a problem in the first place *unless it would benefit other people to know.*

If you need to tell someone you have a problem—do so immediately! But first, think of a solution and start to implement it. Then approach your manager like this:

"Abe, I can't be here next Friday. But because I know others are depending on me, I've already done the report that's due Monday, and I've started the other tasks. I've let Macy, Tracy, and Lacy know I'll be gone, and we've discussed things. I'm sure they'll be fine without me, but I wanted to keep you up to date."

Abe then asks a few questions, which you answer, and then you joke around.

Compare that with this:

"Abe, I'm going to be gone tomorrow, and I'll need someone to cover for me. I haven't written any instructions. Is that okay?"

Abe is going to need aspirin.

But What If I've Done All That, and My Career Is Still Stagnant?

Maybe your boss isn't very observant, or grateful. If that's the case, it's probably time to leave the organization (#6e, *Quit Your Horrible J.O.B. That's Killing You*). Why not go where they appreciate you?

Get a Raise

You'll probably get a 1 or 2% raise every year anyway, but if you want to jump 10% or more, you have to *demonstrate to the leaders that you are bringing in extra revenue or prestige.*

To get a raise, you must view events from the manager's perspective. I have a friend who once saved Sprint over $250,000. Does he deserve a raise? Heck yeah!!!

I asked him if he thought about saying, "Mr. C.E.O., I found a foolproof way to save us $250,000. If you want to know what it is and if it works, I'd like a $50,000 bonus." After all, Sprint would still save $200,000—and make a star employee happy (**Part VIII: The Five Keys to Negotiation**).

He laughed and said, "Believe me, I thought about it!" But he was only 25 and not as bold then as he is now. I'm sure he'd do it now. After all, he doesn't have to work for Sprint; dozens of organizations would benefit from having him.

If you can point to *money saved, incomes increased,* or *improvements to the organization that you've made,* then if times are good overall, they *should* give you a raise!

If they won't, then maybe it's time to *Quit Your Horrible J.O.B. That's Killing You* (#6e).

29. Get a J.O.B. (How to)

You really don't want a J.O.B., which stands for Just Over Broke.

A job is where you don't like what you do, dread Monday mornings, wish you could arrive late, leave early, and do as little work as possible.

J.O.B.s are about the paycheck, which is always too small. Incidentally, a raise doesn't make anyone work harder. People are not solely motivated by money. Would you work twice as hard if they doubled your pay? You may want to, but is that even physically possible?

People with J.O.B.s often are surrounded by unhappy coworkers who do as little as possible, take very little initiative, and have a lot of resentments against other people.

When you think about millionaires, they tend to love their work. After a certain point, they keep going, even though they don't need the money. Someone like billionaire Mark Cuban of *Shark Tank* could have retired just a few decades into his career. But he clearly loves all of his projects.

A J.O.B. is the worst-case scenario. Don't get a job. Discover your *Personal Mission* (#31 & 32), instead, and try to see how your current job can be made to fit it. If your J.O.B. can't be a part of your PM, then *Quit Your Horrible J.O.B. That's Killing You* (#6e).

If you can't quit, then maybe with a little thought, you could transform your current J.O.B. into something that fits your PM. For example, let's say you work in fast food and don't like it. Can you use it to learn:

* Outstanding social skills (#33, *Givers, Matchers, and Takers: Who Makes the Most Money, and Whose Careers Go the Farthest?*)

* Ultra-efficiency? Can you save the organization money (#28, *Get Promoted and/or Get a Raise*)?

* Character building (#27, *Seven Jobs Everyone Should Have, Love, and/or Hate*).

I heard a story about a waitress who was hired on the spot by a PR company because she was so friendly and on-task. On Monday, she was making $2.13 per hour + tips, and Tuesday she gave her two weeks notice and soon was making $40,000+ doing what she always loved. Chances are, when she became a waitress, that wasn't her Dream Job for All Time. She could have easily resented her manager, customers who don't tip, and being stuck with the second shift. She could have spent all her time complaining, and many people would say she'd be right to do so.

But the thing is: you never know whom you're going to meet, and how you could mutually serve each other and the larger public. So, she made the best of things, and now she's living out her Personal Mission.

30. Get a Career (How to)

Careers can be a trap. People go to college and become, say, an engineer because they believe they can make $60,000 to $90,000. In the grand scheme of things, this is not a lot of money *if you're going to be unhappy.*

A lot of people wake up one day when they are 35 years old and wonder—how did I get here? Why is life so boring and unfulfilling? They climbed the career ladder—only to discover that they'd leaned it up against the wrong wall.

The problem with "having a career" is that people sell out for relatively little money and average status.

Take the time to discover your Personal Mission. If you know it, and engineering fits it, then you will be deeply happy, and *Happy People Make More Money* (#66). Conversely, the person who chases the dollar never seems to catch it, and ends up with a miserable J.O.B. (#29).

Equally Bad…

…are the people who say, "Would you rather have money or would you rather be happy?"

That's because it's not how much you make. It's how much you keep! (**Part X: Millionaires Think Differently Than the Middle Class.**)

Dr. Thomas Stanley in *The Millionaire Next Door* found that a lot of teachers, plumbers, firefighters, cops, and others often retired with a net worth of $1,000,000 to $2,000,000+. So, it's a false choice to pretend to choose between money and happiness.

It's even good to ask, "Why do people talk like this in the first place?" Is it because they don't like their J.O.B. (#29)? They should *Quit The Horrible J.O.B. That's Killing Them* (#6e). Especially they should quit if they're in any kind of people profession. If they work around people all day, then the people they allegedly serve should not have to listen to complaints. Be a giver, not a complainer/taker! (#33, *Givers, Matchers, and Takers: Who Makes the Most Money, and Whose Careers Go the Farthest?*)

31. Get a Personal Mission (How to)

A Personal Mission is why you are on this earth.

I recommend that you Google "Other people's Personal Missions" and read. You can also take Personality Tests like the MBTI, as well as Interest Inventories.

My favorite idea? Ask family and friends what you were like as a kid, ages 0 to 12, before the fear of other people's criticisms started to hit. When you were ten years old, you probably just went about your day, having fun, and mostly enjoying yourself. You were probably kind to others, but not too concerned with their opinions of you. You didn't worry too much about what everyone thought. (Our worries about What Will Everyone Else Think of Me?! usually start in junior high. That's when we thought we knew what we wanted to do, but we start doubting ourselves because of fear.)

As a kid, you knew what you liked and did what you liked. Many very wealthy people are still behaving in ways congruent with how they were as kids. I bet Mark Cuban now and Mark Cuban, age 5, are basically the same joyful guy. Everyone said that about Teddy Roosevelt. "You have to remember," said one observer, "that the President is about six."

I hesitate to use myself as an example, but I believe I am here:

a) To love God and brag Him up;

b) To maximize my own potential (heart, mind, body, soul, personal finance, adventure, service, and creative);

c) To help others maximize their potential;

d) To be creative, both artistically and in the creation of events for others to enjoy and benefit from.

If anything you're doing, or any relationship you are in, does not fit your Personal Mission, you may want to think long and hard about whether you should keep going, or choose a direction in better alignment with whom God wants you to be.

When you understand what your PM is, you'll realize that you could probably do 25 different jobs and be 99% fulfilled in each of them. For example, a person who loves science and loves people *might* be a doctor, nurse, PT, OT, psychiatrist, psychologist, pharmacist, hospital administrator, or 18 other things.

Pray about it, and try to make decisions relatively quickly. Often a good way to see if something fits is to actually try it out. For example, maybe you think you want to be a doctor, but have you ever *job shadowed* a doctor? *Taken* a doctor *to coffee* and *played 20 Questions*? If you have no actual experience, then you only have speculation, and that's not actual information.

Here are a few questions to get you started. Pray first, and try to answer them as God might:

a) What types of people, activities, and things have you always loved?

b) Who do you want to help?

c) What do you want to do, even if just once?
d) What would be satisfying?

e) What would be fun?

Try These Things

a) Take one to five Personality Tests.

b) And several Interest Inventories.

c) Ask family to help you re-discover your childhood passions.

Caution

Sometimes, people spend *years* in prayer asking God, "What do you want me to do with my life?"

In *Decisive*, by Dan & Chip Heath, the authors quote a priest who says people always ask him this question; they're looking for life direction. He responds:

"There are probably over 18 things you could do that would make God very happy!"

And the old priest adds, "I think most people go about this question all wrong. They don't say this, but they seem to think that here's what God thinks: 'I know what you're supposed to do, but I'm not going to tell you, even when you ask. *And then I'm going to be angry if you don't follow my will.*"

People should pray for guidance everyday—but why do you think God gives us all of these tools (like re-discovering your childhood, personality tests, and interest inventories) to figure out our Personal Mission if we weren't meant to use them?

32. Get a Personal Mission, Part II: Five-Step Career Process

This is a lot of work, but I think it would also be a lot of fun: take this Process as far as you can until you are crystal clear on your *Personal Mission* (#31).

CAREER PROCESS & Personal Mission: A Five-Step Process That Seeks to Help You Graduate Debt Free and At Peace With Your Choice of Major

a) Take an interest inventory, aptitude tests, (Career you've never heard of), personality test, and write 2 to 3 pages about when you were five.

b) From the above, come up with 7 to 12 options.

c) Take someone to coffee in all 7 to 12 of those fields. Ask each person 20-25 questions.

d) Later that day, journal about the Q & A. On that field, are you a yes, no, or a maybe?

e) Job Shadow all 7-12 of the professionals for at least 3 hours each.

f) See if you can line up an apprentice or internship.

Why do I think this would be fun (as well as beneficial)? Because no one in our society seems to do anything like this. That makes it an adventure.

Over 50% of workers don't like their J.O.B.'s. And over 50% of employers think believe they've made a lot of serious hiring mistakes (#26, *Be Aware That Hiring Processes in America Are Messed Up*). And they have $8,000 in credit card debt on average, a student loan, a car loan, and a mortgage so they can't Quit the Horrible J.O.B. That's Killing Them (#6e).

The problem with the way most people choose their careers and their college major is: they may have very little hands-on experience. Then when they're actually in that situation, they discover for the first time that they don't like it.

What I propose is: when you Job Shadow and/or Take Someone to

Coffee, you will have an emotional reaction. You will love it or hate it. These emotions are what you want! After all, *Happy People Make More Money* (#66).

33. Givers, Matchers, and Takers: Who Makes the Most Money, and Whose Careers Go the Farthest?

Dr. Adam Grant wrote *Give and Take: Why Helping Others Drives Our Success*, in which he researched the four kinds of people. Please Google "Give and Take Quiz" and see which kind you are.

Givers, "Otherish" → Have the best relationships, tend to make the most money, have and enjoy the most success in their chosen fields of life.

Matchers → Practice 50/50 "Give and Take" in most aspects of their lives. They do okay in America. They're the baseline.

Takers → Actually do the second worst. When people realize someone is a taker, they tend to run in the opposite direction. Takers are exhausting. (#79, *Spoiled Brats*). On TV, Takers often make the most money and do the best. But that's TV.

Givers, "Selfless" → Do the worst of all people. That's because they get taken advantage of, and they essentially get bled out, depleted because they think, "That's what good people do. Good people make sacrifices."

Good people *do* make sacrifices—all the time! So, what are the differences?

"Otherish" Givers

* Achieve the best and the most

* Have strong goals for themselves that they are pursuing.

* Give constantly while simultaneously pursuing own goals.

* Think Win/Win or No Deal

* Discern the other person. Is this person a Taker? If so, then the Otherish Giver doesn't reward bad behavior.

* Do what's in the best interest of the other person, which means saying *No* to *all* Spoiled Brats.

* Has a strong conscience.

* Gives constantly, every day, while doing well for themselves. In the end, gives *the most* because they have *the most to give.*

Selfless Givers

* Achieve the least.

* At best, their personal goals are inarticulate—if they exist at all.

* Put their own needs on the backburner, and get used up, exhausted and empty.

* Get caught in Lose/Win situations.

* Starry eyed; wears rose-colored glasses; forgets to love the sinner and hate the sin.

* Worries other people won't like them if they say no.

* Gets guilt-tripped into doing others work for them.

* In the end, doesn't have anything left to give; taken to the cleaners.

Was Jesus an "Otherish Giver"? After all, he was crucified. Doesn't that make him a Selfless Giver?

I think Jesus was Otherish. Jesus pursued all of his own goals by saying everything He wanted to say and healing everyone He wanted to heal. He wanted to change everything, and He did.

Also, because He had more than everyone else—He is God—He gave away more than everyone else by being crucified (and by teaching, healing, and founding Christianity).

He even teaches us how to sacrifice. "Father, if you are willing, take this cup from me; yet not my will, but yours be done." -- Luke 22:42. So, you could say Jesus *voluntarily chose* to be crucified. He could have walked out of the garden.

And Jesus also chooses to resurrect Himself. So, while I am not a theologian, is it fair to say that Jesus is the most influential person in human history? And further, that He accomplished more than anyone else?

He looks infinitely wealthy to me—Jesus has true wealth, and the *most* to give. That fits the profile of Otherish.

34. Get Help, and Help Others

In life, almost everyone needs help. To make good money, ironically, it's often best to act generously. Thus, strive to:

* Be a mentor; mentoring will help *you*. Teachers retain 98% of the information they teach. Mentors must not only know their profession inside and out; they must be able to *explain their thoughts clearly*.

* Find a mentor, even if that mentor lives far away or lived long ago. (See #35, *But Who Can Do You Go for Advice When You're #1?*)

* Be an "Otherish Givers" (#33) because it's deeply moral, satisfying, and fun. Also, you'll make the most money.

Doing these things is an Emotional Intelligence (EQ) skill. The good news is that EQ, according to authors like Daniel Goleman, is highly malleable. With consistent effort, all of our EQs can go *way* up.

35. But Who Can You Go to for Advice When You're #1?

How does Michael Jordan become a better basketball player?

How does William Shakespeare become a better writer?

How does J.D. Rockefeller—the richest man in human history—become a better businessman and philanthropist?

Who do you go to when you're #1? To yourself? Or maybe to the person who is #50?

You need a mentor. Further, understand that *leaders are readers.*

Presidents often read biographies of Abraham Lincoln and Theodore Roosevelt. Popes read the Saints. The founder of Pixar, Inc., (Edmund Catmull) made an in-depth study of Walt Disney, his predecessor, as well as Joseph Campbell (who has a brilliant understanding about how stories work or fail). World-class athletes study other world-class athletes.

Key advice: Read Three Books by Experts and You'll Be an Expert—or Close Enough!

There is a lot of *average* advice out there; seek out expert advice instead. That's why I've done my best in this book to bring you the advice of millionaires.

When it comes to educational systems and results, Finland and South Korea consistently get ranked as tied for #1 across the world; read *The Smartest Kids in the World,* by Amanda Ripley. So, it won't surprise you that—in an effort to improve—the South Koreans are studying the Finns.

If you can't find an expert to talk to, why not read more? Sometimes, the smartest people lived thousands of miles away, and centuries ago.

Cut through the Clutter and Noise of Competing Claims That All Sound Good by Looking Strictly at Results.

When I wanted to get more fit in 2014, I looked at Tony Horton, 55, the creator of P90X because Tony Horton *has results*—look at the man! He's ripped!

Chalene Johnson, 45, is beautiful, so I trust her fitness programs like PiYo and Turbo Fire.

Many Okinawans are literally over 110 years old, and they are gardening and playing with little kids. So, what is their lifestyle? Can I stop doing what I'm doing and start doing what they're doing?

Who has done what you want to do?

* Can you learn everything about their lives?

* Can you read everything they've ever written?

* Can you start to imitate, while keeping your core identity intact?

According to Shane Snow (author of *Smartcuts: How Hackers, Innovators, and Icons Accelerate Success*), brilliantly accomplished people often have mentors, and half the time, the mentor lived long ago. Excellent musicians, for example, might learn everything they can about the life and work of Mozart. Inventors learn everything they can about Thomas Edison.

But the research on mentoring is mixed. Lots of people have excellent teachers, coaches, and managers, but you'd never know it. The only way to truly benefit from excellent mentoring is for the student to simultaneously give it his or her all.

Caution: Many People, Like Family and Friends, Will Tell You That Mediocre Is Good Enough.

When you're #1, a lot of people will say things that you don't want to hear, like "I was happy with making a B," or "Why don't you just relax"?

That's not the advice Michael Jordan wants to hear. Pixar didn't think *Toy Story 2* could be average, but the people above them were okay with it just being average because it would still make money. Pixar didn't listen; they junked the "good enough" draft and started over.

When you're aiming for #1, you don't want to be told that being #5,023 is good enough.

In America, "normal" in financial terms means having $8,000 in credit card debt, a car loan, student loan, a mortgage, and maybe a J.O.B. (#29).

My formula for life is: I love everyone, especially family and friends, but I am seeking out the best mentors. Like Isaac Newton said, "If I have seen further, it is by standing on the shoulders of giants."

36. Work...For Free!

It is often said that middle class people work for a paycheck and wealthy people work to learn. They build their skill set, and are always making themselves more valuable.

Working at a lot of different things with many different people is an adventure. It's too bad more people don't try it. They'd set themselves apart, become more of their true selves, maybe meet all the right people in their chosen fields, figure out *for sure* what they like and don't like, and maybe even get a fantastic job offer (#32, *Five-Step Career Process*).

Working for free could teach you more than an expensive college education. (#23. *Don't Be a Statistic*).

37. The Four Ways to Make Money

They are:

* Employee.

* Self-employed.

* Business Owner.

* Investor.

Each has its advantages and disadvantages, so here is a basic overview:

* For experience in life, try *all four and see what you like the most.*

* For the first two, if you aren't there, you don't make money.

* The last two tend to pay the most and have the most freedom.

* The last two are the only ones where you make money *when you are not there.*

There is no job security anywhere.

People who become Employees sometimes say they want a safe, secure job. There is no such thing. Why not?

+ Technology is moving too fast. Companies rise and fall all the time.

+ The average person switches jobs every 3-4 years.

+ The economy can tumble into recession, and *anyone* can get laid off.

+ Your organization can go out of business and *everyone* gets laid off.

+ If you work for the government, even that might someday shrink.

+ You can love your work, but if you get a new boss, sometimes, that's like *changing employment*. The new boss might be a nasty person, and you may desperately want to *Quit Your Horrible J.O.B. That's Killing You* (#6e).

+ Your life circumstances can change. For example, I've known people who love their work, but the minute they had their second baby, they couldn't take it anymore. Between 40-50 hours at work and two young kids, they were breaking down. So, they quit, and have stayed at home ever since.

Your only real job security is knowing your skills in the marketplace, and increasing your skills.

If you can do what you're doing for one organization, perhaps you can do it for another.

Epic Mistake

One terrible action I believe people take is: they return to college to *pick up a credential*. That is, an advanced degree like an M.A.

Here's what's wrong with that: some of these people are attending college rather cynically, hoping to just get a raise, and not to actually learn anything. "I took this summer class," one of my friends once said, "and it was great! I didn't have to learn or do anything!"

View that conversation from the leader's point of view. (#28, *Get Promoted and/or Get a Raise*). In the race between having a *credentialed staff that isn't educated, has few skills, and has that attitude* vs. *having people who hope to seriously upgrade their skills so as to improve their organization*, the leader will choose the second option.

To be clear: I love college and learning as much as possible. Which means: *As a College Student, Think Like a Millionaire* (#24).

Conclusion: All Four Options Are Good

Employer, self-employed, business owner, and investor: all four options are wonderful! Especially if you are *Working to Learn* (#43).

But which pay the most? If you're successful at them: business owner and investor. But you also have to take your personality into account.

Ultimately, why not do some of each?

Part VI: What Are the

Best Investments?

38. Houses & Real Estate

Dave Ramsey (author of *The Total Money Makeover*) invests in paid-for real estate, and he has a net worth of at least $55,000,000. Robert Kiyosaki (author of *Rich Dad, Poor Dad*) has also made a fortune in real estate—but he follows a very different financial model than Dave Ramsey's. You can read both of their books.

In the meantime, here is a little advice:

* Do the Baby Steps in order. *Do not buy a house outside of this order because a house has at least $5,000-10,000 in extra expenses that people don't describe. Maybe that's because they think you already know.*

* Only buy if you plan on living in that house for five years or longer.

* Read a book on houses first, ask a lot of questions, and educate yourself.

Q. Do you know any real estate agents? Can you take them to coffee, just to learn?

Here's where I'm going to get controversial.

Your house is actually a terrible investment. That's because with taxes, insurance, mortgage interest, repairs, and more, a house can easily cost you more than you'll ever sell it for!

The story in #18 (*Renter, Owner, and/or Landlord?*) illustrates this perfectly. To recap, in *The Wall Street Journal*, I read a story by a family who bought their home for $166,000 and sold it twenty years later for $500,000.

In other words, it tripled in value and they made $334,000, right?

Wrong. Adding up all their taxes, insurance, mortgage interest, and so on, they actually spent $498,500 on their house over those twenty years. And they hardly did any repairs or paintings. And they remodeled nothing.

All told, they made $1,500 over twenty years, which comes to $75 per year.

I pay about $3,000 per year just in taxes, insurance, and maintenance. Over twenty years, that's $60,000, so the family's story makes sense to me. (#18b. *Your House Is Not a Moneymaking Asset*).

But buying a house beats renting.

If you split costs with friends and rent for as little as $300 per month, you will spend $3,600 per year, and that's cheap. Apartment complexes are at least $600 to $900+ per month. You get none of that back. At least the family got their $498,500 back.

You should rent if you are likely to move soon, or if you aren't on *Baby Step* #3d (#4).

But what about owning a house and renting it out?

People make fortunes doing this. A house might just net you $1,000 per month. (The figures vary tremendously, of course.)

The people whom I know do it this way:

* They read books by Russ Whitney (*Millionaire Real Estate Mentor*) and Robert Kiyosaki (*Rich Dad, Poor Dad*).

* They find a mentor who owns 10+ properties him or herself.

* They keep detailed budgets and balance sheets.

* They learn about plumbing, electricity, cement, roofing, siding, painting, and all kinds of repairs. They become Mr. or Miss Fix-It.

* Eventually, their phone has many plumbers, electricians, cement people, roofing companies, and more in their contacts.

Because houses cost so much, the people I know study a lot. I would, too, if I were going to get into this.

39. Growth Stock Mutual Funds

I am going to go out on a limb, here, and say: if you're going to invest in the stock market, you should invest primarily in index funds (See #40, *Index Funds.*)

Most funds have hidden fees. Index funds don't.

Most funds underperform the market averages. Index funds beat anywhere from 55-80+% of the mutual funds out there, almost every year.

In fact, I am going to dangle from the most dangerous limb and tell you what to invest in: probably something by Vanguard, although any index fund with a good track record, very low fees, and a reputation for being 100% honest should do.

Why is telling you what to invest in going out on a limb? It's because most advisors won't do that. After all, what if you lose money? Then whose fault is that?

Well, it's yours. See the **Disclaimer** at the end of this book. We are all responsible for doing our own research and investing our own money wisely. In fact, you will be a better investor if you do.

It's just that the track record is so much better for index funds (since at least 1926) than almost anything else out there as far as I know.

For now, I want to point you toward two essays: one by Dave Ramsey, and the other by Dan & Chip Heath. Here are the bullet points of each:

Dave Ramsey's Plan for the Stock Market

* Invest in growth stock mutual funds – either actively managed, or index funds.

* Skip bonds. Skip individual stocks. Skip options, commodities, and practically every other kind of investment. Their average return is far below 12%, which is what the stock market has averaged since 1926.

Read a) "The 12% Reality" (see the link below, from Dave's website) and b) "The Myth of Mutual Funds" (from Dan & Chip Heath's website), chapter #40.

a) "The 12% Reality" is at:

http://www.daveramsey.com/article/the-12-reality/lifeandmoney_investing/

The key point is: the S&P 500, created in 1926, has average an 11.69% return from 1926-2011. From 2011-present, it's probably higher. Personally, I invest in VFINX (Vanguard 500 Index Fund Investor Shares); it went up about 400% from 2009 to 2019.

b) For "The Myth of Mutual Funds" (from Dan & Chip Heath's website), chapter #40, please see the next chapter for the bullet points, and this link:

http://www.fastcompany.com/966229/made-stick-myth-mutual-funds

I hope it doesn't feel like work to read either of these articles. They're 1.5 to 2 pages long, respectively. I have a friend who read 35 books on investing until he discovered index funds—and pointed out index funds to me. Vanguard Index funds, practically every broker and financial will acknowledge, have a) better performance and yet b) lower fees.

I encourage you to do your own reading about index funds. Warren Buffett put all of his wife's money in index funds. That says a lot.

By the way, why do I tell you what I invest in? For these two reasons, which I mentioned in #4b, (*Do You Know What's Even Better Than the 7 Baby Steps and Budgeting? F.I.R.E.*):

1) Financial advisors who don't disclosure their investments drive me crazy. How do I know if they're any good?

2) You can look these funds up yourself simply by typing their five letters into any search engine. All kinds of graphs and reports will show up.

40. Index Funds (The Stock Market)

Please read: *THE MYTH OF MUTUAL FUNDS: WHY WE DON'T ALWAYS BELIEVE THE TRUTH*

by Dan & Chip Heath, authors of the Brilliant *Switch*, *Made to Stick*, and *Decisive*

http://www.fastcompany.com/966229/made-stick-myth-mutual-funds

The Heaths recommend you buy "boring" index funds. What are these? They are mutual funds that essentially track the stock market.

Since I can't improve upon this short essay (under 850 words) that takes less than five minutes to absorb, I ask that you read it now.

In fact, you can skip everything people hate about investing if you just invest in index funds.

People think investing is too complicated and boring, so they just hand their money over to the nice lady in a suit who talks jargon about 401K's.

Later, people see the market going down and they wonder what happened.

They hear about a new investment strategy and their friend who made 300%, and they don't know why they never get in on those deals.

They are right to wonder.

Eliminate all of these complications and just invest in index funds. Watch your fees go to about .2%, instead of 3% or more. Enjoy the fact that there are no hidden fees. And if the market goes up 10% this year, your fund will go up 10%. Since that is about the historical average, you can count on that, year-in and year-out.

But what if you want to make more than 10%? What if you want to make 100%, or 1,000%? Well, good luck. Mathematicians have tried to beat the index fund; next to no one can do it. It takes time, money, and is not a fun hobby—not in my world. Not when I know the index fund beats 99.9% of mutual fund managers and individual stock pickers.

Still, if you must indulge yourself with stocks, then please see (#41 *Individual Stocks*, #42 *Running Your Own Business,* and the rest **Part VI: What Are The Best Investments?**)

41. Individual Stocks (The Stock Market)

Chipotle debuted in 2005 at $40 a share. In 2014, it was $660 a share—an increase of 1,650%.

Starbucks was under $1 per share in 1993. It was $83 in 2014—an increase of 9,000%.

Apple was $30 in 2010, and $115 in 2014—a growth of 383%.

But how do you pick excellent stocks?

By learning from the best. Two of the greatest investors of the last fifty years—Warren Buffett and Peter Lynch—believe in many of the exact same things:

a) Only buy companies where they make or do something that you *personally* like and understand—or that people you know like and understand. Everyone can understand a burrito. So, when you visit a restaurant, is the food any good? If not, don't buy the stock. That's because a company's stock price must eventually reflect reality. If all of their products are the worst, then the stock eventually will collapse.

b) Only buy stocks in companies where they are already making a profit—don't buy anything on the basis of potential. While you could make a fortune if you guess right, Buffett and Lynch didn't want to guess—they wanted to *know*. (See #48, *Risk vs. Reward*). How do you know if a company's any good? It's already making a profit, and perhaps expanding.

c) Only buy companies with clean balance sheets. Companies that are deeply in debt, for example, are terrible.

d) Buy and hold a stock—never sell it. When the market crashes and your stock goes down by 60% and everyone is freaking out and selling—that's the best time to buy more! You're getting a big discount! When the market revives, good companies often surge the most of all.

Yes, there are exceptions, but Buffett and Lynch don't buy the exceptions.

Read Peter Lynch's book, *One Up on Wall Street,* and you'll see how he does it. It's not too much more involved than what's above, but you should read it. He explains the many ways ordinary investors—people like you and me—can make terrible mistakes, and how to avoid them. You can avoid nearly all of them by never selling the stocks you buy.

Of course, some people say you shouldn't buy individual stocks because they require a lot of time to keep track of. Lynch, however, thinks the average person who works 40 hours per week and has a family can easily keep track of about 8-12 stocks.

Here's what motivates me: if a mutual fund is only going to grow 10% per year and a stock can grow 9,000% in twenty years, that tells me that it's worth it to read a few books by Peter Lynch, get myself informed, and then buy and hold forever. But I've told you enough to get started today.

*   *   *

Short biographies: Lynch's fund at Fidelity made 2,800% over a 14-year period. Warren Buffett is in the top ten wealthiest men in the United States.

Full disclosure: I don't admire Buffett the man, but I do admire Buffett the investor.

42. Running Your Own Business

Apparently, many people with $10,000,000+ don't invest in the stock market—at all!

According to *The Millionaire Mind*, by Dr. Thomas Stanley, the top 1% in the U.S. often believe the best people to invest in is: themselves and their families.

They don't like the stock market because they don't think they really understand it—not really, not in a deep way. Sure, they know what a mutual fund is, and they understand what a share of stock in Chipotle is. But a mutual fund might be involved with 200 separate companies. They don't know what all of those companies are doing.

And even if you buy stock in just one company (like Chipotle), you don't necessarily understand the day-to-day realities. Even if you eat there, you don't know if they're making money, or if a not-smart person just took over the company.

The top 1%, however, do feel like they understand the business that they created.

Take Larry Ryan, of Ryan Lawn and Tree. He created it himself when he was 38 years old. At the time, it wasn't worth anything. But in 2014, they did $24,000,000 in business.

Mr. Ryan understands himself, his partners, his workers, and everything about his business, from how to do what they do to all the numbers. So, he takes the profits and invests them back into his company—in other words, into himself.

That's what the top 1% often do.

In *The Millionaire Next Door*, Dr. Stanley profiled your "average millionaire"—teachers, cops, firefighters, plumbers, electricians, and more middle class people—the person next door who saves and invests, and he found that they often have $1,000,000 to $2,000,000+ by age 65. Those people often *are* in the stock market, and they invest in mutual funds.

But if you want to make a million by the time you are 35 years old, you really need to **Start Your Own Business Now (Part III)**.

Also, please read *The $100 Startup,* by Chris Guillebeau. Here's what amazon.com says:

In preparing to write this book, Chris identified 1,500 individuals who have built businesses earning $50,000 or more from a modest investment (in many cases, $100 or less), and from that group he's chosen to focus on the 50 most intriguing case studies. In nearly all cases, people with no special skills discovered aspects of their personal passions that could be monetized, and were able to restructure their lives in ways that gave them greater freedom and fulfillment.

Guillebeau is an astonishing man: he's visited *every country on earth.* (Sources vary, so there are between 189 and 198, depending on how you count.) I've read his book three times. He certainly understands that future **Millionaires Think Differently Than the Middle Class (Part X)**.

43. Working to Learn

Often, people don't get promoted for doing excellent work. If you do excellent work, they'll think you're in the perfect position! People get promoted when they demonstrate that *they can do someone else's job* (#28 *Get Promoted and/or Get a Raise*).

So learn from mentors (#35, *But Who Can You Go to for Advice When You're #1?*) and read three books by experts in order to become an expert yourself; leaders are readers.

Sometimes, people return to college and get an M.B.A. or another advanced degree. I have mixed feelings about that. In some cases, you will take the greatest courses from the best professors, and it will be a magical period of growth in your life (see #24, *As a College Student, Think Like a Millionaire*).

But it's also expensive, and unless you give it your all, why go? (#23, *Don't Be a Statistic*).

The key question you should ask is: can you teach yourself?

a) Can you read your way into an education?

b) Can you find mentors, both living and historic?

Don't get me wrong: I am in favor of advanced degrees *when they are acquired with the proper spirit*. That spirit is an unquenchable desire to learn (#24).

So, first learn everything you can on your own from books, mentors, and real life experience. (see #31, *Work…For Free*). Then solve other people's problems for them, (#33, *Givers, Matchers, and Takers: Who Makes the Most Money, and Whose Careers Go the Farthest?*) and you'll be happy. And *Happy People Make More Money.* (#66).

44. Having an Incredibly Rare Skill

Are you a(n):

* Professional Athlete?

* Musician?

* Actor or Actress?

* Filmmaker?

* Novelist?

* Nonfiction writer?

* Photographer?

* Influencer?

* Inventor?

* Collector (for example, of baseball cards or rare dolls)?

* Someone who can't be easily categorized?

Advice

* Go for it!

* More than almost anyone else, you *especially* need to follow the Baby Steps (see #3), and more than anything--*avoid debt!*

How will you practice your craft if you have to work an extra 20 hours per week at your second job to pay off your loans?

Questions

* Are you practicing every day?

* Have you read about people like you?

* Who are your mentors, living and dead?

* Is the rest of your life in order enough that you won't have to quit? (#58, *Time*, and **Appendix:** *Time Management.*)

People with rare skills need to be self-starters. That's because these endeavors can be lonely. You must love it enough to be persistent.

Study the experts in your field. The inventors admire people like Thomas Edison or Steve Jobs, and read all about them. The writers read every day. The musicians learn everything about the greats. The videographers buy how-to books no one else they know reads, and they watch instructional videos on YouTube.

A lot could be said about mastering your craft. But to simplify it: practice every day. If you love it, then it isn't about how much talent you already have: it's about how much talent you *develop*.

And understand that your friends and family may not understand what it takes. After all, if you're from a family of engineers or librarians, they may not know just how much an athlete or musician needs to work. They might say, "Relax!" But you probably don't want to relax. (See #35, *But Who Can You Go to for Advice When You're #1?*)

45. Oddities

You can read *101 Weird Ways to Make Money: Cricket Farming, Repossessing Cars, and Other Jobs with Big Upside and Not Much Competition*, by Steve Gillman.

There is a lot to be said for being the *only person willing to do a job*. Not only are you living an adventurous life, you earn people's endless gratitude.

Perhaps Gillman's book will give you ideas for **Starting Your Own Business Now (Part III).**

46. Bonds, Options, Day Trading, and More

You can do what you like, but I would ignore bonds and day trading.

Historically, bonds almost always do worse than mutual funds, which average about 10% per year since 1926 (#39, *Growth Stock Mutual Funds* and #40, *Index Funds*). Since certain stocks can grow by 9,000% (Starbucks, over twenty years), or 1,650% (Chipotle, over five years), why buy something that returns 5% per year, like bonds? (#41, *Individual Stocks*).

Day Trading is essentially gambling. If you master blackjack or craps in Las Vegas, you can win almost 49% of the time. Day Trading is buying and selling stocks (or something else) that morning and hoping it goes up by mid-afternoon. I have a friend who made $10,000 in about a week. The next week, he lost $28,000, which soon was what he owed on his credit card.

Granted, that's only one (horror) story, but with Day Trading, you can't know what you're doing (#48, *Risk vs. Reward*), which means you're not thinking like a millionaire (**Part X**). You're not even thinking like the middle class.

Better Investments

Part III: Start Your Own Business Now

Part IV: Pay for College without Loans

#27. *Seven Jobs Everyone Should Have, Love, and/or Hate*

#31. *Get a Personal Mission (How to)*

#36. *Work...For Free!*

#39. *Growth Stock Mutual Funds*

#40. *Index Funds*

#41. *Individual Stocks*

#43. *Working to Learn*

Bonds do so little. Conversely, Day Trading is the attempt to get something for nothing, and the man who tries to get something for nothing in the long run always appears to pay for it twice over.

47. Being an Employee, Provided You Primarily Work to Learn

Although there are only four ways to make money, one thing that's good about being an employee is: you keep 100% of your income.

Minus taxes. So, maybe 45% of your income, once we subtract federal income tax, state income tax, social security, Medicare, property tax, car tax, sales tax, and many other taxes.

Even so, many employees do very well for themselves. The best paying profession is probably sales (exceeding doctor and lawyer). There are sales people who make over $1,000,000 per year. To do well in sales, you have to love people, be 100% honest all the time, and love your product or service. That's because sales people often have sleazy reputations. The best ones *don't need to make a sale.* Truly, they think long term, about their reputation (#33, *Givers, Matchers, and Takers: Who Makes the Most Money, and Whose Careers Go the Farthest?*)

Other professions can be truly energizing and you will love Monday mornings if you are living out your *Personal Mission* (#31 and #32). You can be in the 40-50% of the population that likes their work (#26, *Be Aware That Hiring Processes in America Are Messed Up*).

Because most people want to be employees, the advantages are well known. So I will sketch a few disadvantages.

Disadvantages

* There really is no such thing as a safe, secure job. People say they want job security, but I know lots of people and have read about fifty stories of people who were doing good/great work, and were laid off in the recession. Or the company went bankrupt. Or the government downsized. Unless you are a tenured college professor or a Supreme Court justice, you truly don't have permanent job security.

* When management changes, that's like switching jobs. A great job can turn into a nightmare within weeks. Maybe it's still "secure," but now it's wrecking your life.

* You don't give yourself raises, time off, work perks, promotions, or any other good thing when you work for someone else.

* You can do great work and never be noticed.

You Will Be Fired

I noticed in my forties that even coaches who win state championships get fired.

In fact, the more I looked around, *anyone* who works from age 22 to 65 will—probably, eventually--get fired. Even if they always do very good work.

Why is this? How can a good person get fired?

Because of bad bosses, office politics, and other events which are simply wrong. Bad things happen to hard workers who work well with others.

That's why you need an Emergency Fund (see #4, *The 7 Baby Steps*), and you should consider a way to *Make $2,000 Using the Skills and Passions You Already Have* (#19).

You should be *Working to Learn* (#43).

It's easy to get complacent. But even if nothing does wrong, routines get boring. And that's no way to *Get Promoted and/or Get a Raise* (#28).

48. Risk vs. Reward

When it comes to investment, the middle class thinks (because they've been told hundreds of times), "the bigger the risk, the bigger the reward."

Mostly false.

In money matters like buying stocks (Starbucks: up 9,000% since 1993), buying index funds (up 10% per year on average since there were index funds), or running your own business—the exact opposite is almost always true.

The more you know about something, the more you *eliminate* risk. Everything in life is this way.

Would you say, "I never study for tests, because going in blind is risky, and the bigger the risk, the bigger the reward!" Or would a coach not bother to examine and plan for the competition as the teams goes into the State Championship?

Every millionaire I've met knows *a lot* about his or her business and investments:

* The farmers worth $2,000,000+ who grew up on farms.

* The stock pickers who studied the companies they bought.

* My thirty-year-old friend who owns 12 houses, who read a dozen books, worked with other landlords, and also picked up everything he can about plumbing, electricity, cement, roofing, and other kinds of maintenance.

Once, I bought 75 copies of a book by an author who has had three #1 national bestsellers. I bought them for $6.95 each and sold them all for a profit of $1.50 to $3.25 each. I really had no risk because if they didn't sell within two weeks, I could return as many copies I liked for a full refund. This is a minor example, but I did what many billionaire investors apparently do: minimized, even eliminated, my downside.

Warren Buffett says his top rule is: don't lose money.

The middle class often invests in mutual funds—and not the index fund variety—where they pay many hidden fees, and they pray for a 10% return. Then the market crashes.

The super-wealthy, however, stay away from things they don't understand, and aim for returns of 100% or more (see #42, *Running Your Own Business*, and the rest of **Part VI: What Are the Best Investments?**)

I love books and have sold many on amazon.com and in other places. Because I know a little about that market, it's easier to eliminate mistakes.

When in doubt:

* Don't invest. Wait.

* Don't invest in anything you don't understand.

* Great investors like Peter Lynch say, "There's never a rush to buy *anything*." (see #41, *Individual Stocks* and **Part XIV: Reading, Viewing, and Online Quizzes** for more about Peter Lynch).

* Seek out no-lose scenarios, like the books I bought.

* Only follow the advice of people who are getting great results (see #35, *But Who Can You Go to for Advice When You're #1?*)

You can't eliminate risk completely. Nothing is guaranteed, not even getting out of bed safely. Anything can happen. That's why you need an Emergency Fund (#4, The *7 Baby Steps*).

Inspiration

Twenty years from now you will be more disappointed by the things you didn't do than by the ones you did. So throw off the bowlines, sail away from the safe harbor, catch the trade winds in your sails. Explore. Dream. Discover. -- Mark Twain

Only those who will risk going too far can possibly find out how far they can go. -- T.S. Eliot

Part VII: Taxes

49. What Millionaires Often Do

* Pay ALL of their taxes IN FULL.

* They DON'T CHEAT.

* They practice fanatical levels of honesty and integrity in everything they do.

* They are generous.

* They hire the best tax professionals possible and pay as little as possible, in accordance with the law. Both liberal Democrats and conservative Republicans millionaires do this.

Character is Destiny. When you cheat to win, you violate **The Five Keys to Negotiation (Part VIII)**. You don't **Think Like a Millionaire (Part X)**. TV millionaires cheat, but TV is entertainment.

Where did I get this information? Dr. Thomas Stanley (author of *The Millionaire Mind*, which is about people who have earned $10,000,000+), who has surveyed thousands of millionaires and studied them for thirty years. Other studies corroborate what Dr. Stanley has learned.

If I were you, I wouldn't believe that millionaires lie, cheat, and underpay their taxes because then, *subconsciously, you'll avoid money*. Because if only bad people become millionaires, why would you want to become a bad person?

I advise you to be fanatically honest in everything you do, because that's even what most millionaires *enemies* say about them: "I don't like that (millionaire) couple. But I have to admit: they are always honest, and they do everything they say they are going to do."

In fact, take integrity a step further and be a rock-star giver. (#33, *Givers, Matchers, and Takers: Who Makes the Most Money, and Whose Careers Go the Farthest?*) God wants you to be a giver (#2, *God and money*).

105

50. Vote

At risk of making people angry, I recommend that 95% of the time, you vote for lower taxes *for everybody*.

Endless books and articles have been written about taxes elsewhere, and taxes play a role in every election, so you can read as much as you like about this. I am simply going to approach taxes from the standpoint of your personal finance.

Like Rabbi Daniel Lapin, author of *Thou Shall Prosper*, I believe that that most people who earn money from work and/or investing do so because they have added that much goodness to the world. So, if you've earned $3,000,000, that means you've added $3,000,000 in goods and services to the world.

In contrast, the American government virtually always borrows and never saves. Next to no one thinks the government handles money well. They are dysfunctional. P.J. O'Rourke says that giving money to government is like giving whiskey and car keys to teenage boys. This is a *Spoiled Brat* problem (#79) and a *Boundaries* problem (#74).

If you think your taxes should be higher, just send the extra in.

I do believe you should tithe (see #2, *God and money* and #33, *Givers, Matchers, and Takers: Who Makes the Most Money, and Whose Careers Go the Farthest?*). If you want to make sure you are handling 100% of your money intelligently, nothing beats starting everything off right with your first 10%.

When would I vote in favor of higher taxes? If World War Three started and our survival were at stake, I'd vote for things I normally consider wasteful: 90% tax rates (like in WWII), titanic levels of borrowing (also like WWII), and infinite spending. Some things—like survival—are more important than money.

On the other hand, another world war would probably involve nukes. After the war is over, paper money will probably be worthless. At that point, the real currency is going to be: food, fuel, shelter, and the relationships you have. So, practice generosity now (#68). Doing so will actually make you happy, and Happy People Make More Money (#66).

Part VIII: The Five Keys to Negotiation

51. The Five Keys to Negotiation

1. Win/win or No Deal.

2. Person with the most information wins.

3. Person who *cares the least* has the most power.

4. Always act with the highest honesty & integrity.

5. If you have enough leverage (good or bad), you can get almost anyone to do what you want.

Some people say that *every conversation is actually a negotiation.* In the sense that both parties want something—whether it's just that someone else listen—this is probably true.

In that sense, we are all negotiating all day long.

Further, sense psychologists estimate that over 85% of all of our satisfaction with life comes from relationships with other people, it's important that we learn how to get along, and to make each other happy. When you look over the ways people interact, where do we mostly live?

The six options are: a) Win/Win or No Deal, b) Win/Lose, c) Lose/Win, d) Lose/Lose, e) Win, and f) Win/Win—Compromise. Let's look at each.

(Btw, I learned of these six options from *The 7 Habits of Highly Effective People*, by Stephen R. Covey. *7 Habits* might just be the greatest personal development book of all time; it's been in amazon's Top 100 books *ever since there was an amazon*, as far as I know.)

a) *Win/Win or No Deal* means we have to communicate fully, love and trust each other, and do our best to make sure we both win 100%. Sounds like a great relationship, right? In business, this would mean both the customer and the seller would walk away happy, and thus prosperous.

b) *Win/Lose* is only good for sports and competitions. Our team wins and their team loses. It doesn't work in business: if you always win and they always lose, they will stop doing business with you, either before or while they go out of business.

Incidentally, some Win/Loses and Lose/Wins are actually Win/Wins. For example, when you think about games, people already know there is going to be a winner and a loser. The loser might be playing a tougher team so as to get better. So, even when they lose, they win.

c) *Lose/Win* means you lose and they win. You will stop doing business with them; they are takers (see #33, *Givers, Matchers, and Takers: Who Makes the Most Money, and Whose Careers Go the Farthest?*). The only time Lose/Win is good is when you are playing a game with a five year old and you let him or her win.

d) *Lose/Lose* is what suicide bombers do: everyone dies. This is like divorce court where former spouses are so hateful that they don't care if they go down as long as their former lover suffers. Lose/Lose is the worst of all worlds.

e) *Win* is when you only care about yourself. It doesn't mean you're against anyone; it's just up to them to look after themselves. This is ultimately a fantasy, because the minute you begin to interact with others, you will either maximize your profit (with a Win/Win) or you will cause hard feelings (a bad Win/Lose) or you will get ripped off (Lose/Win).

Be careful with "Win," because Takers get labeled. (#33, *Givers, Matchers, and Takers: Who Makes the Most Money, and Whose Careers Go the Farthest?*).

f) Win/Win—Compromise. This one isn't bad. You ask for a 20% raise and the boss says, "No raise!" and eventually you settle for 10%. You get a raise and he keeps a good employee. Everyone got *part* of what they want.

But could you have made it a Win/Win or No Deal? What if you held out for the whole 20%, provided you brought in more profit for the company? Bring in enough extra profit and you'll deserve a 100% raise! (#28, *Get Promoted and/or Get a Raise*).

Ideally, you'd use all five keys in every negotiation. While I believe they're self-explanatory, I recommend practicing with family and friends. Especially pay attention to #4, Always act with the highest honesty & integrity, because if you lie, you'll get a terrible reputation, and that makes every future negotiation a lot harder. For more, read *Character* (#70).

52. All Relationships Thrive Under These Conditions

We should aim for a Win/Win or No Deal in all of our lives. Otherwise, we'll be struggling (and probably failing) to work with anyone from the dishonest to people who don't communicate. And the good news is: Win/Win or No Deal fits more than business.

Literally millions of books have been written about love, friendship, and all other relationships, and I'm no relationship expert.

Even so, imagine all of your relationships as a Win/Win or No Deal. Who wouldn't want a romance, a family, a friendship, and a partnership where both parties always sought to do what was in *the best interest of the other person?*

Try This

Re-envision any relationship where you are dissatisfied. Mostly, is it a) Win/Win or No Deal, b) Win/Lose, c) Lose/Win, d) Lose/Lose, e) Win, or f) Win/Win—Compromise?

Can you shift it to a Win/Win?

Or should you renegotiate or end the relationship?

53. But Don't Women Hate to Negotiate?

I've heard this, and it's been my experience that a lot of women—and a lot of men—all say they hate to negotiate. I don't know if disliking negotiation is a female thing.

I believe that's because too many people aren't thinking Win/Win or No Deal (#51 & #52). They are thinking negotiation is supposed to be nasty, deceptive, and ultimately a dirty power struggle. That's what that word means to many people, even though that's not what the dictionary says.

The basic idea behind Win/Win or No Deal is:

* Both sides get 100% of what they want.

* Totally open communication: it takes awhile to talk out what everyone wants.

* 100% trust.

* Some creativity: you might have to do some intelligent imagining if you want to work out how both sides can be happy.

Please read pages 206 to 214 of *7 Habits of Highly Effective People.* Stephen R. Covey's book has been a national bestseller since he published it in 1990—and that's because it's so good about relationships (and life).

If you get the feeling that the other person isn't being open or honest, you must have the courage to call him or her out on it. If they won't come clean, then this isn't a time to be a victim (Lose/Win) or to crack their skull (Win/Lose). It's certainly not time to make a *Spoiled Brat* (#79) worse; dishonest people already have problems with *Boundaries* (#74). It's time for No Deal. While walking away, pray for them, and let it go. Tell them that you'll resume the relationship when things are Win/Win.

Part IX: When You're On

a Losing Streak

54. What Coaches Do

When a team starts losing, the coach calls, "Time out!"

The players are rattled. Or their strategy is off. Or both. So the coach interrupts the losing streak.

After you quit, you can pray, rest, change the subject, get advice, and otherwise recharge your heart, mind, body, and soul.

Did you know that psychologists have proven that if you meditate every day, there are measurable health benefits? Meditation is good for the soul—and your psyche. Many millionaires like Tim Ferriss (author of *The 4-Hour Work Week*) meditate every day. Tim Ferriss flunked high school Spanish, but he learned it later, and by age 30 was fluent in six languages.

Caution: you must set a deadline for re-entry. Some people quit and never return—but they meant to. If you dare, ask older people this question: "Is there anything really important to you that you quit and meant to return to, but never did?"

They may not tell you their story; it might feel like a major failure to them. But if they have the courage to be honest, and if they deeply love you, they'll tell you the truth: quitting something you love feels rotten.

Always do the Rocking Chair Test. That's when you picture yourself at the age of 100 sitting in a rocking chair and looking back on your life. Are you going to be happy that you went for it (whether it worked out or not)? Or are you going to be ashamed that you didn't have the courage to try?

Part X: Millionaires Think Differently Than the Middle Class

55. Key Differences

Millionaires think long term.

The middle class pays lip service to thinking long term.

Millionaires talk about ideas.

The middle class talks about things and other people.

Millionaires embrace change.

The middle class is threatened by change.

Millionaires take calculated risks.

The middle class is afraid to take risks.

Millionaires continually learn and grow.

The middle class thinks learning ended in school.

Millionaires work for profits.

The middle class works for wages.

Millionaires believe they must be generous.

The middle class believes it can't afford to give.

Millionaires have multiple sources of income.

The middle class has only one or two.

Millionaires focus on increasing their net worth.

The middle class focuses on increasing their paychecks.

Millionaires ask themselves empowering questions.

The middle class disempowering questions.

-- From *The Top 10 Distinctions Between Millionaires and the Middle Class*, by Keith Cameron Smith.

May I add…?

* Millionaires look at true value. Two examples: #11, *Cars*, and #24, *As a College Student, Think Like a Millionaire.*

* The middle class thinks it must pay more than it actually has to. It often buys new.

* Millionaires often notice what everyone else is doing, but don't follow along. They believe if you do what everyone else does, you'll end up like everyone else.

* The middle class conforms. Often this conformity is *subconscious*, even *instinctual*. No one likes to be labeled a conformist who can't think for him or herself. But we all look around us for social cues to see what we are supposed to do, especially in new situations.

* Millionaires think like investors, owners, and creators.

* The middle class thinks like consumers.

* Millionaires plan ahead, sometimes years ahead.

* The middle class often stops planning after it goes to college.

* Millionaires think houses are either neutral items or liabilities—and certainly not assets! That's because they define an asset as something that puts money in your pocket. Houses take money out. (See *#18b. Your House Is Not a Moneymaking Asset*).

* The Middle Class Thinks Houses Are an Investment

* Millionaires *Work to Learn* (#43), and even *Work…For Free!* (#36).

Even if you don't become a millionaire, you can simply reread the statements and you'll realize that that's a better mindset to have. It's the mindset of someone who has a crystal clear *Personal Mission* (#31 and #32).

55b. Many Millionaires Avoid Sophistication

I don't mean they "avoid reading books" or that they are anti-knowledge (See #35, *But Who Can You Go to for Advice When You're #1?*). What I mean is: be like Albert Einstein, who said, "Everything should be made as simple as possible, but not simpler." By all means: get as much education as possible!

But I think most millionaires can do their budgets on one sheet of paper, the envelope system, or they use a simple app (#6a, *What It Looks Like*).

And they don't do things like this!

* Having a student loan maybe at 5%, and then taking a lot of cash and investing it in the stock market while hoping to make 10%. 10 – 5 = 5%, right? Sophisticated "investors" say they just made 5%--and they used other people's money to do it!! (They say) they're brilliant!! Right?

These scenarios almost never play out this way.

You think you'll make 10%, but what about when the market goes down that year, and everyone's investments actually lose 10%? When that happens, -5 – 10 = -15%. If you invested $1,000 like this, you just lost $150.

Second, *people forgot about taxes*. You can easily lose 3% on anything you make, so even if you made 10%, now subtract 3% for taxes and 5% from the interest, so you just made 2%. In this scenario, where you invested $1,000, you just made $20. Seriously?! You just risked $1,000 to make $20.

Some people risk their whole house this way. They borrow $100,000 against their house in an effort to make 10%, or $10,000. But when the market goes down, they lose $1,000 to $40,000 instead, like in 2008.

Third, people seldom factor in the *time* they waste investing all that borrowed money. How many hours did it take to choose those investments and send in the money—to strangers—so they can invest it for you? Wouldn't you have made more if you were *Working to Learn* (#43)?

Finally, people almost never take how emotionally exhausting and mentally taxing it is to play the games of sophistication. They borrow money to invest, and every moment spent doing that is a moment that could have been spent with family, friends, or doing something else more beneficial.

But what about ordinary situations, like buying *Cars* (#11)? In short, the more "sophisticated" you get, the more apt you are to get lost in a maze of payments where you get drowned in numbers by experts, and seduced into buying fancy extras that you didn't even know existed until the car salesperson points them out.

Don't get lost in a blizzard of "sophistication." Many millionaires only invest in one or two things (See #42, *Running Your Own Business*), and they like to keep it simple because they don't like investing in what they don't understand (#48, *Risk vs. Reward*).

56. But Aren't Most Rich People Jerks, Entitled, or Spoiled Brats?

In America, 99% of us *are* the rich people.

In a world where 1,000,000,000+ people live on $1 per day and another 1,000,000,000+ live on $2 per day, and we have a Third World that we could rename the *Two-Thirds World*, we are the rich people.

So, aren't we the entitled spoiled brats? After all, most of us have food, heat, AC, electronics, and free access to public libraries. Other people often have no food at all.

That's why I think it's important to be a giver (#33, *Givers, Matchers, and Takers: Who Makes the Most Money, and Whose Careers Go the Farthest?*) I am sure that "The Lord Loves a Cheerful Giver!" (2 Corinthians 7:9).

Specifics According to Several Researchers, Including Dr. Thomas Stanley, Who Has Studied Millionaires for over Forty Years

1. First Generation Rich

Many first generation millionaires are teachers, police officers, firefighters, electricians, engineers, and others who work hard for a living and live modestly. He found many who never made more than the median income in America. They never buy new cars, and they live in middle class neighborhoods because they are aware of the phenomena where people actually do spend more if they live in "wealthy" neighborhoods: statistically speaking, people really do try to "keep up with the Jones." We all think we're independent thinkers, but subconsciously, if we're not careful, we often just do what everyone else is doing. So many first generation millionaires live by average people so that they don't overspend. Essentially, in many ways, they look middle class. (From *The Millionaire Next Door*.)

Also, Dr. Stanley found that millionaires often have very little in common with each other—they are all kinds of different people—but they frequently do share these traits:

* They possess sky-high levels of honesty and integrity. Even their enemies who hate them will admit that they are *very* honest people—maybe the most honest people they know.

* 87% married a very supportive spouse. (see #77, *Marriage.*)

* They tend to be more religious than average.

* They are generous (#33, *Givers, Matchers, and Takers*)

In short, real millionaires do not behave like TV millionaires. (From *The Millionaire Mind*, also by Dr. Stanley.)

2. Second Generation Rich

Apparently it is often the case that when they are continuing their parents' business, they often make it bigger and better. Mom and Dad got it started…the kids make it HUGE.

3. Third Generation Stumble

Unfortunately, people have chronicled that the third generation can often be lazy and entitled. Sometimes, they party all of the money away.

But now that this pattern is well documented, it appears that some wealthy families are taking this into account. They don't want to raise *Spoiled Brats* (#79).

Raising children is infinitely complex, but it appears that the key is: even if your family has $100,000,000, *every child must have responsibilities and deadlines, with few exceptions.*

One of my students at UMKC, 21, was studying to be a doctor. She was rich and brilliant. Her family took her skiing in the Swiss Alps and they jetted around the world. She had never had a job other than making straight A's.

But she also woke up at 6 a.m. and studied eight hours per day, six

119

days per week. She truly wanted to be a doctor, and her parents gently but firmly provided the necessary discipline until her habits were natural to her.

While I hope that you work all *Seven Jobs That Everyone Should Have, Love, and/or Hate,* (#27), it's not necessary that you get paid to do them. You just need to do them. After all, Character is Destiny.

Part XI: The Rest of Your Life

(Will Either Make You Rich or Make You Angry)

57. Sheer Laziness and/or Sick of It All

It's worth asking: when you're lazy or burnt out, is it actually your fault?

I do believe you should *do everything that you say you're going to do*. That's part of **Thinking Like a Millionaire (Part X).**

But it's equally true that the hardest workers almost always tend to love what they do. Michael Jordan practiced basketball two hours a day longer than anyone else—is there any doubt that he loved basketball?

If you are lazy, should you *Quit Your Horrible J.O.B. That's Killing You* (#6e)? Should you seriously re-examine your *Personal Mission* (#31 & #32)?

When You're On a Losing Streak, you should call, "Time out!" **(Part IX.)**

My advice is: use the 80/20 Principle (described in *The Best Way to Shop* in the **Appendix**) to clarify your commitments, fulfill *all* of them, and then step back and look at the big picture of your life. Are you overworked? Because not all overwhelmed people are *Spoiled Brats* (#79).

But I must add: it's important that you solve your burnout soon—because others *perceive* burnt out people as unreliable. Which means it's hard to get raises, promotions, or even a good reputation. If I were you, I'd view this as a crisis to solve, not a feeling of overwhelm from which you must escape.

58. Time (and Self-Management)

* The Big Picture on time management involves knowing what your Dreams and Goals are. You may want to do a dream session, like Matthew Kelly's team does, as he describes in his entertaining little book, *The Dream Manager.*

* Through all of this, hopefully you've clarified for yourself your *Personal Mission* (#31 & 32).

* Now you're ready for actual time management. That's where Stephen R. Covey's Habit #3: "Put First Things First" comes into play. In the **Appendix,** I outline the best method: planning by the week with your major roles in life in mind.

59. Space: Your Physical Environment and Your Stuff

How does cleaning up your physical space and stuff save you money? A happy environment leads to a happier life, and psychologists have proven that, generally speaking, *Happy People Make More Money* (#66).

And we all have things we don't like or need that we could sell (#5, *The Three Quickest Ways to Have More Money: Income, Expenses, and Selling Stuff*).

People actually pay Professional Organizers large amounts to help them straighten up. I've read two authors who have made fortunes: Julie Morgenstern and Marie Kondo. Their advice is brilliant. Here are just five tips:

1. Do Pile-SPACE, as Morgenstern outlines:

Sort them.

Purge things you don't like, need, or will never use.

Assign a Home for every item.

"**C**ontainerize" them.

"**E**qualize." In other words, do it again every six months.

2. Use the Kindergarten Classroom

Julie Morgenstern uses this on everyone, from multi-million dollar executives to stay-at-home parents.

Ask yourself, what is this part of the room for? For example, in a Kindergarten Classroom, there's a reading corner, an arts and crafts corner, a food corner, and more.

The reading corner only contains reading things: a rug & beanbag, a shelf, and a lamp. People who are messy do not naturally do this: they might have clothes and kitchenware mixed together. This method saves you time and makes things tidy.

3. Read The Life Changing Magic of Tidying Up, *by Marie Kondo.* This short guide is actually fun. I can see why this author's description from amazon is true:

Marie "KonMari" Kondo runs an acclaimed consulting business in Tokyo helping clients transform their cluttered homes into spaces of serenity and inspiration. With a three-month waiting list, her KonMari Method of decluttering and organizing has become an international phenomenon. *The Life-Changing Magic of Tidying Up* is a best seller in Japan, Germany, and the UK, with more than two million copies sold worldwide, and has been turned into a television drama for Japanese TV.

I will give you Marie Kondo's best tip.

4. Does It Spark Joy?

Marie Kondo first has you declutter all of your possessions, once and for all, in one shot. It may take six months. Then she says, *you never have to do it again for the rest of your life.*

How can she claim this, and also say that none of her clients have ever reverted to their old ways?

Because she only wants you to keep items that "spark joy."

Start with clothing. Put everything in one pile. Then, as you pick up each item one at a time, as yourself, "Does this give me joy?"

If it doesn't, out it goes.

Recommended: read the whole book and outline your plan before you tidy a single thing.

5. *The Best Way to Shop* (**Appendix**) ultimately involves taking inventory, organizing everything in that category, discarding, and then making a plan...all before you buy anything! If you follow *The Best Way to Shop*, your wardrobe (or whatever category of life you are dealing with) will be sleek and organized, and it will "spark joy."

60. Hoarders

You're probably not an addict or have a serious mental illness, which is what some hoarders have fought losing battles with. I knew a lady who never threw away anything. You couldn't walk into any of the rooms of her house—everything was packed to the ceilings. Eventually, she bought the neighbor's house and started filling that.

If you just have too much stuff, then you might be lucky. Free money! (#5, *Selling Stuff*).

To sell stuff, read #59 *Space: Your Physical Environment and Your Stuff*, and #61, *Annoying Things*. As you start to streamline, you will get just a little happier. And *Happy People Make More Money* (see #66).

Ironically, I advise you to borrow or buy just one more thing: *The Life Changing Magic of Tidying Up*, by Marie Kondo. You will love this startlingly simple, easy, energetic book. Why not read the first 20 pages for free on amazon?

61. One Hundred Annoying Things

Being stressed out is bad for your finances. Stress leads to expensive means of trying to get rid of stress. Americans:

* Eat too much high calorie, no/low nutrient food;

* Drink too much;

* Smoke too much;

* Gamble too much;

* Spend too much;

* Watch TV too much; and

* Surf the web too much;

All but the last two cost us money *immediately*, and more cash in the long term. Every moment spent wasted on TV or online is time that could have been spent with family or friends, or *Working to Learn* (#43). Said another way, because time is money, wasted time is wasted money.

So, try this tip from *Coach Yourself to Success,* by Talane Miedaner:

* Make a list of everything in your life that annoys you. The average person's list is actually *90 to 120 items long.*

* Systematically work to eliminate *everything* on that list.

You might eliminate over half of them just through rethinking your *Space: Your Physical Environment and Your Stuff* (#59).

62. Alcohol

Alcohol costs money, of course. Adults can probably afford a drink, but alcoholism and/or any addiction will destroy most people's money supply. If not now, almost always over time.

A few people might be rich and an alcoholic, but these stories almost always have depressing endings. Read or view the story of one of my favorite authors, F. Scott Fitzgerard (*The Great Gatsby*), who died of a heart attack at the age of 44. Further, even when he was making $1,000,000 a year (in the 1920s, when a dollar was worth at least ten today), the author and his wife, Zelda, were spending at least $1,300,000. Alcoholism led them to caving into every whim.

If you are an alcoholic, nothing I say will change your mind, so this section is more for people who know alcoholics.

Advice

* You cannot change them.

* Read *The Big Book of Alcoholics Anonymous*, and anything else you like about addiction. Even if you don't know any alcoholics, anyone who is interested in people, psychology, or literature should want to understand the nature of addiction.

* Go to an "open meeting" of Alcoholics Anonymous. AA (and many other organizations like NA, GA, OA, DA, and more) sometimes let anyone attend. If you want to learn more in an hour than many adults learn in six months (or even six years), you should attend one.

* For the addict, their behavior is simply more important to them than God, you, their family, friends, their health, and their wealth.

* They must consume larger amounts all the time, although the highs get smaller.

I've supported my friends by attending Al-Anon meetings with them, and I've read a few books on addiction. It is one of the ugliest currents in

American life.

In money terms, all I can say is: addicts will easily cost you all your money. They will betray you, and make your life hell, and then promise you that tomorrow everything will be better when it will actually be worse. They can't help it. They're in the grip of a powerful force.

When it comes to addicts, I don't know whether to tell you to "be careful" or to just run. If you can give them your friendship and prayers *and never your money under any circumstances*, that would be ideal. But the moment you become emotionally entangled, you will enter a world of early sorrow and poverty.

63. Pitfalls of This Decade (and the Last, and the Next)

If you want to be healthy and wealthy and wise, like Benjamin Franklin was (a happy inventor, genius, and entrepreneur who left millions of dollars to the two cities that he loved), then it helps to be *wise*.

Don't Be a Statistic (#23). Instead, think about *Who Can You Go to for Advice When You're #1?* (#35).

Maybe we live in a stressful country. I do know most of these pitfalls will limit your happiness and wealth:

* The Standard American Diet, or SAD (#64, *Health and Nutrition*);

* Credit Cards, because *Debt Trips Up Your Opportunities* (#8);

* *Car* Loans (#11);

* *Student Loans* (#22);

* Being credentialed but not educated (*Get Promoted, #28,* and *Working to Learn, #43*);

* Distractions and multi-tasking;

* TV;

* Keeping up with the Jones (**Part X: Millionaires Think Differently Than the Middle Class**);

* Glitzy surfaces, and status-seeking vs. underlying realities (#24, *As a College Student, Think Like a Millionaire*);

* "For whatever I'm suffering from, there must be a pill" (and not a long-term solution);

* Toxic Relationships (#74, *Boundaries*, and #79 *Spoiled Brats*);

* Trying to buy things that should be free: love, friendship, and much more (#6h, *Increase Your Fun While Paying Less*);

* Unclear priorities (#31 & 32, *Personal Mission*); and

* Putting God anywhere but first (#2, God and money).

Advice

Make a list of the biggest ten time-wasters and *fake stress relievers* in your life, and then systematically eliminate all of them from your life. Often, it feels just as good to stop doing something painful as it does to start doing something joyful.

64. Fitness and Nutrition

The sooner you take total control of this aspect of your life, the sooner you will minimize:

* Medical bills that can be anywhere from $100,000 to $500,000;

* Extra insurance costs;

* Time away from work being sick, which costs you money and promotions (#28, *Get Promoted and/or Get a Raise*).

Close to 70% of all Americans are at an unhealthy weight, and every major disease (heart attacks, stroke, cancer, diabetes, and literally 94,000 more) are up by 30-44% since 1960. Given how technology has advanced, Americans should be getting healthier, but this generation of people under the age of 18 is projected to *have shorter lifespans than their parents.*

What people seldom think about it: your ability to think in a lightning fast, crystal clear way like a superhero is enhanced by excellent nutrition, while junk food often wipes people's mental whiteboards blank. But how can you miss all of the ideas you *didn't* have because you were powering your brain with junk food and "carbage"?

From a monetary angle, your brain is your #1 asset. But in our very unhealthy country with the Standard American Diet (SAD), sick is normal, so people don't realize what they are doing to themselves. But on some level, everyone knows that you are what you eat.

Perhaps because I was a donut-loving six-year-old who was 20 pounds overweight when most of the other boys weighed 70 pounds in first grade, I've since embarked on an incredible research project. I've seen over 23 documentaries and read major portions of 20-40 books. I've even given a presentation, "In Search of Ideal Nutrition," over five times to 140 people.

Advice

I cannot outline entire nutrition programs here, so I will just tell you which exercise systems and nutritional plans I like. If I were you, I'd borrow any beachbody.com program (like "P90X" or "21-Day Fix"), and I'd consider going Paleo, Whole 30, Keto, or Carnivore. Personally, I've been 95-99% Paleo (with 1-5% cheating) since March 2015. On it, I've ran two 26.2 mile races (marathons), lifted weights three times a week, done thousands of sit-ups, and felt my energy level stay strong and steady. I endorse it, but since I don't know your situation, I urge you to do your own research.

Bon appetite! As your thinking grows crystal clear, and your taste buds reset to crave healthy food (and dislike unhealthy substances), you will make more money, and that's in part because *Happy People Make More Money*, #66.

65. Wealthy and Unhappy?

The media loves to show unhappy wealthy people. It makes for fascinating drama, and on some level, perhaps it makes a few people living paycheck to paycheck feel better. But some wealthy people *are* unhappy.

Who are they?

* Sometimes, Third Generation Rich Kids are miserable (#56, *But Aren't Most Rich People Jerks, Entitled, or Spoiled Brats?*).

* And often—studies show—lottery winners are less happy a year after they win than they were before. Unless they roll their windfall into *The 7 Baby Steps* (#4), they tend to do things like quit their jobs and go on vacation. This is a life devoid of purpose—no *Personal Mission* (#31). For almost adults, "no purpose" equals misery.

Perhaps this explains why many lottery winners eventually end up broke. They quit work and indulge themselves, of course, and may get sloppy with their lives. But deep down, they aren't happy, and *Happy People Make More Money*, #66. In their misery, perhaps on some level they seek to "get back to normal," and in America, normal is broke.

66. Happy People Make More Money

From *Scrum: The Art of Doing Twice the Work in Half the Time,* by Jeff Sutherland:

Happy people do better—at home, at work, in life. They make more money, have better jobs, graduate from college, live longer. Almost universally, they're better at what they do.

They sell more stuff, cost less, leave their jobs less, are healthier. Happiness leads to success in nearly every domain, including marriage, health, friendship, community involvement, creativity, and in our jobs and businesses.

A meta-analysis of 225 papers with over 275,000 participants found that people who felt happy were more likely to secure job interviews, be evaluated more positively, show superior performance and productivity, and be better managers.

Intuitively, it makes sense that happy people do better—it's because of their success that they're happy, right? Wrong. From the same meta-analysis: "Study after study shows that happiness precedes thriving."

That's right. People aren't happy because they're successful; they're successful because they're happy.

And performance improves even if people are only a bit happier. You don't have to change people's lives dramatically to make them happier, at least temporarily. Even just a little leads to markedly better outcomes. People don't have to be deliriously, wedding-day happy, just a little happier than they were. Even small gestures can have great impact.

One thing happiness is not: complacency.

Scrum is a great book; you'll love it.

It's important to understand this, because our culture promotes a lot of myths (of course).

They say, "Money can't buy you happiness," but this commonplace saying is flawed at best. When we take care of others and improve our own wellness, we feel satisfaction. For example, buying groceries for their families makes people happy.

Further, psychologists have proven that *when you give money away*, you get a boost of happiness. People who tithe also feel connected and loved in their church.

And people who move from barely surviving to subsistence report increased happiness.

Finally, people who *earn* a million dollars report increased levels of well-being, but people who win the lottery tend to be *less* happy a year later. Why is that? Because it's more about what you've accomplished and how you manage your life, not about what you have. (#65, *Wealthy and Unhappy?*)

A final note: while psychologists have shown that happy people tend to make more money, money itself does not *guarantee* happiness. Rather, when people are happy and accomplished, they tend to *thrive*, and thriving means overall improvement, and that often has a financial component.

So be happy: you'll make more money.

67. Avoid the Happy Trap

Happy People Make More Money (#66). But there's a complication. *Scrum* author Jeff Sutherland points out that researchers were forced to drop the word "happy" when for some people, it connoted complacency. If you're predisposed to be a lazy person, you misunderstand what psychologists think of as happiness. You think happiness means *doing as little as possible.* But laziness isn't happiness; it could be purposelessness. And it's the opposite of **Thinking Like a Millionaire (Part X).**

So, Sutherland discovered, researchers and efficiency experts were forced to replace the word "happy" with "thriving" because of how complacent people were misunderstanding it. But even lazy people can understand that when you do nothing, you might feel somewhat okay right now, but you aren't thriving. And it won't be long before you let down the people close to you.

68. Generosity

Most millionaires-to-be are generous, but the middle class believes it can't afford to be generous (**Part X: Millionaires Think Differently Than the Middle Class**).

Dr. Adam Grant, a sociologist, wrote *Give and Take: Why Helping Others Drives Our Success.* In it, he explained how people from President Lincoln to the lead comedy writer at *The Simpsons* reached the top through their incredible giving—and they weren't "buying affection." They truly gave from the heart. (See #33, *Givers, Matchers, and Takers: Who Makes the Most Money, and Whose Careers Go the Farthest?)* Lincoln even lost an election in which he had the lead because he thought the other man would do a better job.

Not only do generous people tend to make more money—and achieve greater success in everything they try—they also tend to be happier, and *Happy People Make More Money* (#66).

You can practice generosity in two ways:

* Work your way up toward tithing, which means to donate 10% of your income to worthy causes (#2, *God and money.*)

* 24/7, be courteous and kind, and see if you can identify and cheer up the loneliest person. Since what gets measured gets managed, it probably helps to make a chart and keep track of how many good deeds you do. Otherwise, it's easy to overestimate how many kind actions you've actually performed. Human beings, in general, tend to be atrocious time, money, and kind-action estimators.

69. Gratitude

Most people know that grateful people do better in life than people who complain endlessly. They live longer, have closer relationships, and just enjoy everything more. They even manage tragedy and crises better. Ultimately, grateful people are happier, which gives them the zip they need to solve life's problems.

And being in the right mindset will help you do better with money, of course. People who are very upset tend to do something in a dysfunctional way, whether its to become a shopaholic, eat too much, drink too much, smoke, gamble, work too much, procrastinate, or otherwise self-sabotage (#63, *Pitfalls of This Decade* and 64. *Fitness and Nutrition*).

Perhaps *all* self-destructive behaviors are subconscious attempts to make a person feel better. The problem is: you can't get enough of what you never needed in the first place.

But just telling people, "Be more grateful!" is like yelling at a nervous wreck to "Relax!"

Fortunately, you can Google "gratitude exercises" and at least 22 specific practices will appear. You don't have to settle for a pep talk. You can use actual science to be more grateful, and thus more happy. Remember that *Happy People Make More Money* (#66).

But I must give one warning: some people take gratitude too far. That is, they do not see life in a whole way. Their artificial happiness and deep suppression of facing facts is actually the opposite of gratitude: it is fear.

70. Character

"Character is Destiny." -- Aristotle

It's worth noting that while millionaires often have very little in common, they are known for their sky-high levels of honesty and integrity (#56, *But Aren't Most Rich People Jerks, Entitled, or Spoiled Brats?*). Sometimes, they *Work…For Free!* (#36). They are generous (#33, *Givers, Matchers, and Takers: Who Makes the Most Money, and Whose Careers Go the Farthest?*) They behave the way most people do who *Get Promoted and/or Get a Raise* (#28).

Many people don't believe this. They say, "*But Aren't Most Rich People Jerks, Entitled, or Spoiled Brats?*" (#56). Some are, but less than you'd think (#65, *Wealthy and Unhappy*).

So, what constitutes good character? In short, my friend Cora Caitlyn keeps getting promotions simply by *doing everything she says she's going to do. (Debt Trips Up Your Opportunities,* #8).

Honesty, responsibility, and generosity: start with these, and work your way up. And whether you're a man or a woman, I believe the people who give the most love do so because—no matter how tough things get—they embody the most courage.

71. Peak Performance

When you want to be #1, my advice is: *stop asking 99% of the people around you for tips on how to be the best.* Instead, find out who actually is #1, and go to that person (#35, *But Who Can You Go to for Advice When You're #1?*) If that person lives far away or lived long ago, like Mozart, then read everything you can about your new mentor.

And in the meantime, there are several books by peak performance coaches. Read at least one:

Finding Your Zone, by Michael Lardon.

Less Than a Minute to Go, by Bill Thierfelder.

Mind Gym: Achieve More by Thinking Differently, by Sebastian Bailey

Mind Gym: An Athlete's Guide to Inner Excellence, by Gary Mack and David Casstevens

10-Minute Toughness: The Mental Training Program for Winning Before the Game Begins, by Jason Selk.

Advice

Don't just read: implement!

Practice the 80/20 Principle, which I outline in *The Best Way to Shop* (**Appendix**).

72. Unexpectedly, the Bible Has a Lot to Say about Money

If God talks a lot about money, it must be because money is important. Here are more nuggets about money, work, and relationships, and generosity from Dave Ramsey's website:

Proverbs 21:20

"In the house of the wise are stores of choice food and oil, but a foolish man devours all he has."

Proverbs 13:11

"Dishonest money dwindles away, but he who gathers money little by little makes it grow."

Luke 14:28-30

"For which of you, intending to build a tower, does not sit down first and count the cost, whether he has enough to finish it, (29) lest, after he has laid the foundation and is not able to finish it, all who see it begin to mock him, saying 'This man began to build and was not able to finish'."

Matthew 6:24

"No one can serve two masters. Either he will hate the one and love the other, or he will be devoted to the one and despise the other. You cannot serve both God and money."

Luke 8:14

"...but as they go on their way they are choked by life's worries, riches and pleasures..."

Proverbs 6:6-8

"Go to the ant, o sluggard, observe her ways and be wise, which, having no chief, officer or ruler, prepares her food in the summer, and gathers her provision in the harvest."

Romans 13:8

"Owe no one anything except to love one another, for he who loves another has fulfilled the law."

Proverbs 21:5

"The plan of the diligent lead surely to plenty, but those of everyone who is hasty, surely to poverty."

Proverbs 29:15

"The rod and reproof give wisdom, but a child left to himself brings shame to his mother."

Proverbs 22:6

"Train up a child in the way that he should go, and when he is old he will not turn from it."

Proverbs 27:23

"Be diligent to know the state of your flocks, and attend to your herds."

Proverbs 16:3

"Commit your works to the Lord, and your thoughts will be established."

Genesis 41:35-36

"And let them gather all the food of those good years that are coming, and store up grain under the authority of Pharaoh, and let them keep food in the cities. Then that food shall be as a reserve for the land for the seven years of famine which shall be in the land of Egypt, that the land may not perish during the famine."

Proverbs 28:20

"A faithful man will abound with blessings, but he who hastens to be rich will not go unpunished."

Psalms 62:10

"...if riches increase, do not set your heart on them."

Proverbs 24:27

"Prepare your outside work, make it fit for yourself in the field; and afterward build your house."

Psalms 20:4

"May He give you the desire of your heart and make all your plans succeed."

Isaiah 30:1

"Woe to the rebellious children, says the Lord, Who take counsel, but not of Me, and who devise plans, but not of My Spirit, that they may add to sin."

Matthew 6:21

"For where your treasure is, there your heart will be also."

Genesis 2:24

"Therefore a man shall leave his father and mother and be joined to his wife, and they shall become one flesh."

Ephesians 4:2-3

"With all lowliness and gentleness, with long-suffering, bearing with one another in love, endeavoring to keep the unity of the Spirit in the bond of peace."

I Timothy 5:8

"But if anyone does not provide for his own, and especially for those of his household, he has denied the faith and is worse than an unbeliever."

Proverbs 29:17

"Correct your son, and he will give you rest; Yes, he will give delight in your soul."

Proverbs 23:13-14

"Do not withhold correction from a child, for if you beat him with a rod, he will not die. You shall beat him with a rod and deliver his soul from hell."

II Thessalonians 3:10

"For even when we were with you, we commanded you this: If anyone will not work, neither shall he eat."

Proverbs 16:31

"The silver haired head is a crown of glory, if it is found in the way of righteousness."

Proverbs 11:1

"A false balance is an abomination to the Lord, but a just weight is His delight."

Galatians 5:22

"But the fruit of the Spirit is love, joy, peace, patience, kindness, goodness, faithfulness."

Proverbs 22:26-27

"Do not be one of those who shakes hands in a pledge, one of those who is surety for debts; if you have nothing with which to pay, why should he take away your bed from under you?"

Psalms 109:11

"Let the creditor seize all that he has: and let strangers plunder his labor."

Proverbs 11:15

"He who is surety for a stranger will suffer for it, but one who hates being surety is secure."

Psalms 37:21

"The wicked borrows and does not repay, but the righteous shows mercy and gives."

Proverbs 6:1-5

"My son, if you have become surety for your friend, if you have shaken hands in pledge for a stranger, you are snared by the words of your own mouth; you are taken by the words of your mouth. So do this, my son, and deliver yourself; For you have come into the hand of your friend; Go and humble yourself; plead with your friend. Give no sleep to your eyes, nor slumber to your eyelids. Deliver yourself like a gazelle from the hand of the hunter, and like a bird for the hand of the fowler."

Ecclesiastes 11:2

"Give portions to seven, yes to eight, for you do not know what disaster may come upon the land."

Proverbs 27:12

"A prudent man sees evil and hides himself, the naïve proceed and pay the penalty."

James 4:14

"...for what is your life? It is even a vapor that appears for a little time and then vanishes away."

Proverbs 13:22

"A good man leaves an inheritance for his children's children, but a sinner's wealth is stored up for the righteous."

I Corinthians 9:9

"Don't muzzle the ox while he is treading out the grain."

Matthew 10:16

"Behold, I send you out as sheep in the midst of wolves. Therefore be wise as serpents and harmless as doves."

Proverbs 10:22

"The blessings of the Lord makes one rich, and He adds no sorrow with it."

Proverbs 14:29

"He who is impulsive exalts folly."

Proverbs 1:5

"A wise man will hear and increase in learning, and a man of understanding will acquire wise counsel."

Proverbs 31:10-11

"Who can find a virtuous wife? For her worth is far above rubies. The heart of her husband safely trusts her: So he will have no lack of gain."

Nehemiah 5:3

"There were also some who said, 'we have mortgaged our lands and vineyards and houses, that we might buy grain because of the faminie'."

Ecclesiastes 6:7

"All the labor of man is for his mouth and yet the soul is not satisfied."

Colossians 3:23

"And whatever you do, do it heartily, as to the Lord and not to men."

Proverbs 23:4-5

"Do not overwork to be rich; because of your own understanding, cease! Will you set your eyes on that which is not? For riches certainly make themselves wings; they fly away like an eagle toward heaven."

Proverbs 3:27-28

"Do not withhold good from those to whom it is due, when it is in the power of your hand to do so. Do not say to your neighbor, 'Go, and come back, and tomorrow I will give it.' When you have it with you."

Proverbs 19:21

"Many are the plans in a man's heart, but the counsel of the Lord, it will stand."

Proverbs 22:1

"A good name is to be chosen rather than great riches, loving favor rather than silver and gold."

Ecclesiastes 5:5

"It is better not to vow than to vow and not pay."

Matthew 5:40-42

"And if anyone wants to sue you, and take your shirt, let him have your coat also. And whoever shall force you to go one mile, go with him two. Give to him who asks of you, and do not turn away from him who wants to borrow from you."

Psalms 50:15

"Call upon me in the day of trouble: I will deliver you, and you shall glorify me."

Philippians 4:6-7

"Be anxious for nothing, but in everything by prayer and supplication, with thanksgiving, let your request be made known to God; and the peace of God, which surpasses all understanding, will guard your hearts and minds through Christ Jesus."

Philippians 4:19

"And my God shall supply all your needs according to His riches in glory by Christ Jesus."

Psalms 24:1

"The earth is the Lord's and the fullness thereof;..."

Deuteronomy 26:12

"When you have finished paying all the tithe of your increase ..."

Genesis 28:22

"And this stone, which I have set up as a pillar, will be God's house: and of that Thou dost give me I will surely give a tenth to Thee."

Matthew 23:23 and Luke 11:42

"Woe to you, scribes and Pharisees, hypocrites! For you pay tithe of mint and anise and cumin and neglected the weightier matters of the law: justice and mercy and faith. These you ought to have done, without leaving the others undone."

Ezra 1:4

"...together with a freewill offering for the house of God..."

II Corinthians 9:7

" ...for God loves a cheerful giver."

Malachi 3:11

"And I will rebuke the devourer for your sakes, so that he will not destroy the fruit of your ground, nor shall the vine fail to bear fruit for you in the field, says the Lord of hosts."

I Corinthians 13:3

"And if I give all my possessions to the poor, and if I deliver my body to be burned, but do not have love it profits me nothing."

Luke 18:11-12

"The Pharisee stood and prayed thus with himself ...I give tithes of all that I possess."

Leviticus 27:30

"And all the tithe of the land, whether of the seed of the land or of the fruit of the tree, is the Lord's. It is holy to the Lord."

Deuteronomy 14:22

"You shall surely tithe all of the produce from what you sow, which come out of the field every year."

Malachi 3:10

"Bring all the tithes into the storehouse, that there may be food in My house . . "

Nehemiah 10:38

" ...bring up the tenth of the tithes to the house of our God, to the chambers of the storehouse."

Malachi 3:8

"Will man rob God? Yet you have robbed me! But you say, 'In what way have we robbed You?' In tithes and offerings."

Malachi 3:10

"Bring all the tithes into the storehouse, that there may be food in My house, and prove Me now in this, says the Lord of host, 'If I will not open for you the windows of heave, and pour out for you such blessing that there will not be room enough to receive it."

How we handle money says a lot about how we handle life. Are we generous? Content with what we have? Efficient? Willing to save for the future when the bad times come? Do we plan ahead? Do we learn from our mistakes?

God wants to help you. Ask Him for wisdom, iron will, and help.

Part XII: Family, Friends, and Spoiled Brats

73. Define the Relationship

Is your relationship a Win/Win or No Deal (#51)? Are you with a *Giver, Matcher, or a Taker* (#33)? Have you internalized *The Five Keys to Negotiation* (#52)?

Only you can decide if a relationship should come to an end…but are you surrounded by *Spoiled Brats* (#79)? Would you recommend that *anyone else* get into a Lose/Win or Lose/Lose relationship?

Anything other than Win/Win or No Deal may damage your ability to do well in every other area of your life. It can easily hurt your career and savings, but—even worse—it can poison the rest of your relationships by adding anxiety to your day.

Perhaps as much as 85% of our happiness comes from our connections with other people. Are other people helping you be happy? Are you helping others to be happy?

Relationships cost money—and money is usually the *least* of what they cost.

74. Boundaries

Kind-hearted people sometimes have a hard time saying no—even when they are unwittingly getting taken advantage of by *Takers* (#33), and living in a Lose/Win world (#51).

Conversely, some strong people sometimes don't say yes—even when they know they're too rigid and judgmental. They have "super-boundaries," which means no one gets in, but that only makes them lonely.

Either way, they should read *Boundaries* by Dr. Henry Cloud. I've listened to a lot of the Dave Ramsey Show, and he frequently recommends this book to people whose 35-year-old children are still living in their basements like characters out of the movie *Failure to Launch.*

People with poor boundaries often get taken advantage of in an effort to be kind, but they end up creating *Spoiled Brats* (#79). This is not good for the Brat, although spoiling them seems like a good idea at the time, like giving an overweight ten year olds an ice cream cones because they are begging. But what if the kids get diabetes?

When you create a monster, No Deal is in order. (#51).

Money books aren't supposed to be manuals on friendship, romance, parenting, friendship, and sports teams...or are they? Can people and relationships really be this simple? Aren't they infinitely complex?

People and relationships *are* rich and varied, and yet we can all grasp the concepts of:

* Win/Win or No Deal.

* Turning a good kid into a brat doesn't do the kid any lifelong favors.

* Having *open and full* conversations.

* Calling people out on their dishonesty if they won't do a Win/Win. You don't ever have to pretend that everything's all right. Losing money in these situations is bad, but it's usually just a symptom of much worse personal problems.

Ask Yourself:

a) *What would happen if you simply never paid for someone who has crossed a boundary?*

b) *Are you saying yes out of fear, and not out of generosity?*

c) *If the relationship blew up, in six months would you really miss it?*

The quality of your life will be determined by the quality of your decisions. It's ironic that in the United States, other than the Pros/Cons list and Catholic Discernment, there are actually few popularized processes for making outstanding choices. So, I hope I can help you **Make Better Decisions (Part XIII)**.

Advice

Believe that clarifying healthy boundaries will not only do wonders for your self-respect, it will make you more realistic and save you a fortune.

Go for a perfect situation, described last:

a) A "sturdy boundary" keeps bad situations out; they bounce off.

b) A "boundary hole" is bad. There are two kinds: a) Where others invade your territory and take from you, and b) Where you worry about things over which you have no control.

c) Too much of a boundary is a "wall," which is also bad. That's when people act like North Korea and don't let anything in or out—including good people and situations. Don't be North Korea—while nothing bad gets in, nothing good gets in, either. North Korea is starving to death.

A *perfect situation* is when our entire boundary is made up of "doors" which can open or close depending upon whether other people (or the situation) is being Win/Win with us. We open for Win/Wins; close for Lose/Wins.

75. Nobody Likes a Critic, So When Should You Be Honest?

Employers, in part, promote people who have good personalities (#25, *Get Hired: Job Interviews*). And *generous* (#68) people make more money because they are *givers* (#35). But sometimes, we know the truth about another person—and we hate to admit it.

We feel bad. Maybe we're friends with, or dating that person. So whenever a negative thought about that person occurs to us, we push it away.

This is your conscience fighting with your intuition. Your conscience tells you not to judge people, to love everyone, and to give everyone a second chance.

Your intuition says you're getting mistreated.

Without going too far into psychology, *Boundaries* (#74), or being *Win/Win or No Deal* (#51), let's cut through all the stories and special cases and just make a simple financial point:

Just don't spend any money on *Spoiled Brats* (#79). You aren't doing them any favors. You're making them into worse people—and wasting money!

Instead, show love and friendship in a thousand different ways that are free. Don't give people a fish, as they say. Teach them to fish so that they can be self-sufficient.

It can be tricky to love people 100% (which is following your kind-hearted conscience) while simultaneously taking off the rose-colored glasses and seeing people exactly for who they are. But *the best* parents do it every day. They love their kids completely, but they also understand all of their kids' weak spots and breaking points.

Outstanding coaches do this, too: they know exactly when to take a player out of the game. They still like the player, and want him (or her) to do well—which is why they're taking the player out. It's a Win/Win for everyone on the team.

True leaders know exactly what their team is—and is not—capable of.

Financial advice:

* Spend NOTHING until you've gotten creative first (#6h, *Increase Your Fun While Paying Less*).

* Love the sinner and hate the sin.

* If the other person is truly a Spoiled Brat, sooner or later, they will come looking for something for free—from you. Don't give it. Be an "Otherish Giver," not a "Selfless Giver (#33). That's the best you can do for everyone.

This advice might be hard for some people to hear. They'd prefer to think that the person who is taking advantage of them—the person who is always in crisis—is their true friend. But ask yourself—if the roles were reversed, would that person run to your rescue? Are you the strong one? Are they the weak one? Or do you have a true friendship?

Let your honest intuition be your guide. Sometimes, conscience means you give love, conversation, and engagement—not just cash to get that person past the moment. Because if that person never learns, you're actually making their life worse.

76. Dating

Without getting too far into who pays for what and at what stage of the romance, it is probably fair to say these two things:

Money Can't Buy You Love

I think we all know people who have spent a fortune that they didn't have trying to impress someone who ultimately was not impressed. Men might spend too much on dates, and I've seen women buy a special outfit for just that one special evening—only to never wear that dress again.

It's a test of your creativity and sense of fun to see how many adventures you can have for under $5 a day. It's probably safe advice to say that your date will want to know: are you fun to be around? And are you only fun if you spend money?

If your love interest wasn't all that impressed in the first place, spending a fortune won't change that.

I think we all know people who just radiate energy, and everywhere they go, they don't need money to bring people happiness. What do they do? Can you learn from them without compromising your true self? Ultimately, you want to be *your* best. Not an imitation of anyone else, and not your second best.

Relationships Shouldn't Be 50/50; They Should Be 100/100.

While love is infinitely rich and varied, and no two romances are alike, it's good to ask: if your goal is to get married, what kind of person do you want to marry? A spoiled brat? Or maybe a person who you always have to struggle to win over? Are you looking for a Win/Lose? Or perhaps the martyrdom of a Lose/Win?

Several elderly, happy couples told me that their happy marriages shared five traits. Both people had to be able to:

* **Talk** things out fully (with no running away from difficult topics);

* **Work** (not necessarily at a career, but just in general);

* Make **sacrifices**;

* **Commit unconditionally** to the marriage, because if you think divorce is an option, you'll probably eventually get divorced. That's because in a 50 year marriage, all the bad days *will* add up to at least one horrific year; and

* **Have fun**. Some couples forget that marriage should be fun! Are you bringing any fun? You don't want to be in a boring, loveless marriage.

Without these five facets, the happy elderly couples all tell me that you are marrying a child. A spoiled brat might be a blast to date, and have wild adventures with, but divorce will cost you at least 67% of your net worth, plus 50% of your future earnings—whether you're the man or the woman (#78, *Divorce*).

77. Marriage

87% of all self-made millionaires have a very supportive spouse.

Dave Ramsey tells the story of the two Belgian horses. A Belgian horse is gigantic, like a Clydesdale. One of them can pull 8,000 pounds.

So, you'd think two could pull 16,000 pounds, but on the first day they've met, together they can pull 24,000 pounds. Wow!

And after they've been working together for awhile like old friends, they can pull *32,000 pounds!*

Old people like to say about marriage, "It's easier in life when two horses are pulling in the same direction."

When spouses don't work together, they undermine each others' plans and are stressed out over finances all the time.

Once, I decided to list on paper the five couples I admired the most. Were they support each others goals? Were they highly responsible? And yet did they know how to have fun? Were they seeking to improve their hearts, minds, bodies, and souls?

Excluded: people who complain excessively about their spouse.

Which five couples do you respect the most? Why?

78. Divorce

I believe divorce costs you anywhere between 67% to 100% of everything you have.

After the initial 50/50 split—if it is 50/50--divorce lawyers and court costs are expensive, as is time away from work.

Further, people who are getting divorced tend to be anxious and have a hard time concentrating, which makes it difficult to do well at work. I wonder how many salespeople who are divorcing manage to charm their customers—probably very few.

If you're not in sales, when your productivity drops (due to your distractions and despair), how unhappy will your manager be? Will you keep your job?

Given that 87% of all self-made millionaires have a *very* supportive spouse, and given how much divorce can shake you up, is it possible to say that divorce takes *more* than 100% of your money? (I'm looking at future promotions, greater income, and what would happen if you invest that income.)

Divorced people often suffer ill health, as well, which is pricey. Stressed out, they easily stumble into the *Pitfalls of This Decade* (#63).

The bottom line: divorce is to your current finances *and maybe future potential* what the delete key is to the best essay you ever wrote. If you can avoid divorce, you should.

79. Good Kids & Spoiled Brats

In *The Millionaire Mind* by Dr. Thomas Stanley, after doing literally thousands of surveys of millionaires and multimillionaires, a *common pattern* emerged regarding the children of millionaires. This story says it all:

Once there were two daughters. For whatever reason, the parents treated one as though she were strong, and the other as though she were weak.

When the strong one had a cold, the parents said, "Go to school." When the weak one felt ill, the parents let her stay home.

When the strong one made bad grades, the parents made her study for months until she raised those grades, and didn't let them slip again. When the weak one did poorly, the parents decided it couldn't have been even 1% her responsibility.

By age 40, the strong one was happily married with good kids, making her own money (except for when she chose to stay at home with her little kids), and she was at peace and having fun.

At 38, the one that was perceived by her parents as weak was divorced, unemployed, and scared to death that her parents would cut off the $70,000 they still gave her every year.

Dr. Stanley found hundreds of cases just like this. Inadvertently, the parents had taught the "strong" daughter to be honest and to work hard, and they'd taught the "weak" daughter to be dishonest, manipulative, a quitter, and unreliable.

Because character is destiny, traits that help in the marketplace, and investing, include:

* Honesty and integrity; &

* Self-discipline, generosity, and more.

Spoiled Brats don't get the chance to develop these traits because doing so is uncomfortable. Instead, for them, it's all too easy to fall into the *Pitfalls of This Decade, #63.*

Part XIII: Make Better Decisions

80. WRAP Is the Best Way to Go

The two best books I ever read on making decisions were *Decisive* by Dan & Chip Heath and *In the School of the Holy Spirit* by Fr. Jacques Philippe. I urge you to read both.

Decisive points that that outside of Catholic Discernment, there are almost no decision-making processes in the United States. This makes life harder than it needs to be.

In the School of the Holy Spirit claims it can *teach you to listen to the voice of the Holy Spirit in your life*. In other words, God can guide 99% of your decisions. I believe Fr. Philippe backs up this gigantic claim. (In only 70 pages!)

I start with WRAP because it helps you eliminate most of the terrible decision-making processes we have in the United States, such as:

* Making "Whether or not" decisions;

* Using the pros & cons list (fatally flawed by the confirmation bias)

* Impulsivity;

* Lack of planning for the three or more possible outcomes that all decisions have; these include yes, no, and maybe.

Instead, here is WRAP:

Widen Our Options → Generate five to seven options for any major decision.

Reality Test Our Assumptions → Don't just speculate or analyze something; actually

test your ideas by doing something.

Attain Distance Before Deciding → After a little action and experimentation, sleep on

it. Don't make snap decisions.

Prepare to Be Wrong → More brainstorming, like in **W**, but this time, it's for when

your great plans either work out worse than expected—or better than expected!

Advice

I read *Decisive* about six times and tried to internalize it. Essentially, the book points out that brilliant people, like President Eisenhower often mapped out six courses of action for any given problem. Given all that thought, he tended to make brilliant decisions. After all, he beat Hitler, won two landslides, and guided America through a decade of peace and prosperity.

So, please read the book!

81. Win/Win or No Deal & the Other Four Keys to Negotiation

Remember the *Five Keys of Negotiation:*

1. Win/Win or No Deal

2. Whoever Has the Most Information Wins

3. Whoever Cares the Least Has the Most Power (also called "Walk away power")

4. Always Act with the Highest Ethics & Morals

5. If you have enough leverage (good or bad), you can get almost anyone to do what you want.

Alternatives

1. **Win/Lose** → Only acceptable in competitions. But is it really win/lose? The losers know going in that they might have a "learning experience." It's only a game. Play ball!

2. **Lose/Win** → Only acceptable when you *want* to lose, like when you play ball with a five year old. When I give 10% to charity, maybe that's a "loss" for me because I give up 10% of all I have, but I doubt it; God appears to reward generous people (Malachi 3:15; *Give and Take* by Dr. Adam Grant).

3. **Lose/Lose** → Never acceptable. This is the person who is having a bad week who wants to make everyone else unhappy because misery loves company. Cheer up, Emo Kid. The sun will shine again someday.

4. **Win (and don't worry about anyone else)** → Mathematician John Nash actually proved with game theory (*A Beautiful Mind*) that you'd actually win more if you tried to help the whole group win, not just secure your own ends. So, "Win" doesn't do as much for you (or anyone) as "Win/Win or No Deal."

5. **Win/Win with Compromise** → You get half of what you want;

so does the other side. That's only 50% each. But with Win/Win or No Deal, if you talk it through long enough with high trust, high cooperation, and high creativity, it's usually possible to for everyone to get 80 to 100% of what they want.

Make It Personal

1. Think of the last five interactions (or financial transactions) you had that bothered you.

2. Classify each one as W/W, W/L, L/W, or L/L.

3. Now rewrite each one as a Win/Win or *No Deal.*

Problems

Q. The other side is dishonest.

A. Walk away.

Q. The other side is uncreative.

A. Insist that you sit down for five minutes, use WRAP, and "Widen Your Options" to five or six alternatives.

Q. The other side wants to strong-arm you.

A. Unfortunately, as a teen, I'm sure adults *have* strong-armed you. Enlist other adults (perhaps your parents) to help you.

Q. You think you just have to sit back and take it.

A. That's Lose/Win → You lose, they win. Unacceptable. Change your victim mindset. Go back to the beginning of this section and read through it again.

Q. You've tried everything and you really *do* have to sit back and take it.

A. As soon as possible, write out your objections and:

a) Have an honest conversation with the troublemaker;

b) Get help from trusted others;

c) Find a new job, new club, or new whatever as soon as possible, and QUIT because of Win/Win or **No Deal.**

d) If you are cracking under the pressure, you must:

1. Take excellent care of yourself (prayer, sleep, water, food, etc.), and

2. Radically change the situation.

82. Use Assertive Language, and *Almost Never* Use Dominant or Passive Speech and Writing

Assertive Language involves:

+ Asking for what you want in clear, simple English. For example, "May I go to lunch at 12:30?" "May I retake the test for a higher grade, up to 75%?" "May I have a raise?" Notice that you should say "I" first, and follow it up with a verb.

+ Being able to say no with no hard feelings.

+ Being able to hear no with no hard feelings.

Dominant Language is good when you are the leader, but you must be careful.

+ Be a leader, not a boss. A boss thinks about himself; a leader thinks about everyone.

+ Give clear instructions.

+ What's the plan?

+ Are you flexible?

+ Do you know enough?

+ Are you experienced enough?

Passive Language is good when you are accepting *legitimate* authority. For example,

+ When a good parent tells a good kid what to do, and the kid says okay.

+ When a good senior leader athlete tells underclassmen what to do, and they say okay.

+ In clear hierarchies, like the military.

+ Good leaders know how & when to be good followers.

+ When God tells you what to do (or not do).

The Dangers of Using the Wrong Language

Dominant Language includes:

+ Criticism, which everyone hates.

+ Complaints, which are form of bonding among some friends, but not fun for anyone outside the group.

+ Being a boss, not a leader. That is, being on a power trip.

+ Being emotionally volatile so that everyone is scared of you (and thus doesn't really respect you).

Passive Language includes

+ Never knowing what you want, which frustrates everyone around you. For example, picture this conversation:

Q. What do you want to do?

A. I don't know. What do you want to do? -- *People find both the Q & the A frustrating.*

Getting walked on by dominant people who are taking things (like your time, property, or self-esteem) that they shouldn't have.

Problems

Q. What's a good way to phrase difficult situations?

A. "I don't know how to say this politely or gently, so I'm just going to say it. I want…."

Q. What if I don't know what I want, and thus don't know if I should be assertive, dominant, or passive?

A. 90 to 99% of the time, you should be gently assertive, and let the other person also assert. But for times when you are indecisive: a) Go pray and b) Use *WRAP* (#80).

Part XIV: Recommended Reading and Quizzes

The Bible. Contains at least 72 (some say 438) timeless principles for handling money.

The 4-Hour Work Week, by Timothy Ferriss. Loaded with great ideas for efficiency.

The $100 Startup, by Chris Guillebeau. Ideal in case you want to start your own business. Every person in the book made a minimum of $50,000 per year and started for somewhere between free and $600. The average person: $374.

Read everything by Chris Guillebeau, and listen to his ten-minute podcast, *Side Hustle School.*

101 Weird Ways to Make Money: Cricket Farming, Repossessing Cars, and Other Jobs with Big Upside and Not Much Competition, by Steve Gillman. Fascinating.

America's Cheapest Family, by Steve and Annette Economides. Contains many specifics regarding everything most families do: how to save a fortune on food, fuel, housing, clothing, vacations, and more. Steve and Annette have five kids, made very little money, and still paid off their house in nine years—all while very much enjoying life.

Boundaries by Dr. Henry Cloud. Not a book about money, per se, but about relationships, and the need to keep them straightforward, where everything essential always gets said.

Coach Yourself to Success: 101 Tips for Success, by Talane Miedaner. Simple, effective advice for eliminating the negative in your life in order to maximize the positive.

Creativity, Inc., by Edmund Catmull. Catmull founded Pixar, and knows a lot about business, people, and creating fantastic art.

Decisive, by Dan and Chip Heath. In the top two books of all time for making excellent decisions.

The Dream Manager, by Matthew Kelly. This short novel a compulsive read, and will help you write the best bucket list possible—and act on it.

Financial Peace University, a nine week course by Dave Ramsey.

Give and Take: Why Helping Others Drives Our Success, by Dr. Adam Grant. If you've always believed that it's better to give than to receive, you should read this book. Givers do indeed do the best in our society—but if you give the wrong way, you'll get taken advantage of, and you'll do the other person a disservice by giving them things that worsen their character and personality.

The Life Changing Magic of Tidying Up, Marie Kondo. Wouldn't it be great if everything you owned, and your home, car, and property all *sparked joy*? Translated into 20 languages because Kondo's methods make people happy, and none of her clients have ever reverted to their old ways.

The Millionaire Next Door, by Dr. Thomas Stanley. Dry reading, but it explains how people with $1,000,000 to $2,000,000+ got that way.

The Millionaire Mind, by Dr. Thomas Stanley. How do people with $10,000,000+ think and act? This book explains how, although I find the prose style tough to read.

Millionaire Real Estate Mentor, by Russ Whitney. My friend who went from owning zero to 12 houses swears by this book. He bought his first house when he was 23 years old.

The New Coffeehouse Investor, How to Build Wealth, Ignore Wall Street, and Get On with Your Life, by Bill Shulltheis. The subtitle says it all.

One Up On Wall Street, Peter Lynch. The best stock picking advice from one of the greatest investors of all time.

Organizing from the Inside Out, by Julie Morgenstern. Great advice on streamlining any kind of room or space.

A Random Walk Down Wall Street, by Burton Malkiel. A classic guide to investments, Wall Street, how things really work, and more. First published in 1973 and updated ever since, it's wisdom is timeless.

Rich Dad, Poor Dad, by Robert Kiyosaki. Controversial for many, this book helps many people consider for the first time some very startling ideas about life that have worked wonders for Mr. Kiyosaki and his many devoted fans.

Scrum: Do Twice the Work in Half the Time, by Jeff Sutherland. Scrum conceives of team work in a completely new way. They use it in Silicon Valley, where their technological breakthroughs make people into billionaires and completely change our world.

The Seven Habits of Highly Effective People, by Stephen R. Covey. A national bestseller every year since 1990, this book has improved many lives.

Smartcuts: How Hackers, Innovators, and Icons Accelerate Success, by Shane Snow examines in detail the commonalties between some of the greatest successes of all time, from George Washington and Abraham Lincoln to brilliant inventors like Thomas Edison. Gives the inside track on how brilliant innovators behave.

Stop Acting Rich, by Dr. Thomas Stanley. Simple, clear, and excellent advice, based on many true stories. I am not sure why, but of all Dr. Stanley's books, this one was the most fun to read.

Switch: How to Make a Change When Change Is Hard, by Dan and Chip Heath. When changes are easy to make, we just make them. This book is for all the other changes that individuals—and teams—would like to make.

The Top 10 Distinctions Between Millionaires and the Middle Class, by Keith Cameron Smith. Short and sweet; philosophical.

Total Money Makeover, by Dave Ramsey. Takes anyone from deep debts to millionaire status.

Online Quizzes

"Give and Take Quiz" by Adam Grant

"Grit Test" by Angela Duckworth

Note: *None* of these authors are paying me to promote their work. Instead, I am highly grateful to them for their fantastic work. They've made my life tremendously better. I hope you benefit from their work, too.

Appendix

19 Exercises

Hourly Job! And Scholarships!

Both Are Awesome!

1. Your friend Heather works at Johnny Jims (they compete with Subparway) and starts at $10.00 per hour. Forget that number, because over time, she gets raises—so for the last year, let's say she averages $11.00 per hour.

* * * <u>So use $11.00 an hour.</u> * * *

a) She works 10 hours per week for 36 weeks (during the school year). How many hours is that, and how much money is that?

b) She works 40 hours per week during the summer and vacations for 14 weeks. How many hours is that, and how much money is that?

c) She doesn't work at all for two weeks (Christmas + vacation). How many hours is that, and how much money is that? Hint: When you don't work, how much do you make?

c') Working for others means when you don't work, you don't

_____.

c") However, when you invest, or own a business, when you sleep, eat, go on vacation, read a book, or go on vacation, you still _____.

d) Let's go back to Heather. How much did she make in the entire year?

e) Now take away 10% of what Heather made due to taxes. That's probably too little, but let's be optimistic. So, how much did she make for the entire year?

2. One of your friends went to college where tuition + room + board + books + other expenses comes to $20,000 per year.

a) One friend gets through in 4 years. How much is that?

b) Your other friend is like 75% of all American college graduates—and gets through in five years. How much is that?

3. Heather applies for a lot of scholarships. Her college gets completely paid for. So, how much should her student loan debt be when she graduates?

Hint: don't overthink this question.

4. So, Heather saved a lot of money. Had she made that much money, she'd probably have to give 30% of it to the government for taxes. So, how much is that?

5. *Conclusion*. At their jobs, Heather made _____ in one year. And by getting scholarships, she avoided spending _____ for college. So, having a job is _____ and yet getting scholarships is more _____.

6. Now let's discuss Heather's friend, Mark, who doesn't work and didn't apply for any scholarships. He goes to the exact same school. When he leaves at age 23, he has $50,000 in student loan debt (because his parents covered half of his costs).

Use a search engine and choose a "student loan calculator, and put in: $50,000 for the loan amount at 5%. Pay it off over 10 years.

a) How much is the monthly payment?

b) How many payments is that in months?

c) How many years is that?

d) What is the total Mark paid for his education? (Interest + principal).

e) How old is Mark when his debt is gone?

7. List five things Mark might not have been able to do while he was paying off this student loan debt that you personally might like to do.

a)

b)

c)

d)

e)

8. Now Mark wants to invest. Use this:
https://www.daveramsey.com/blog/investment-calculator/#/entry_form

Mark can invest $1,000 a month until age 70. He invests in various stocks and mutual funds that average 7% because he never heard about index funds.

How much does Mark have at 70?

9. Meanwhile, Heather were investing $500 a month since age 22. She invested in index funds (9.5% return.)

How much does she have when she is 70?

10. So, Heather each made _____. Mark made _____. Both maybe did okay.

11. What are your ideas about this?

18 Again

Assignment

1. List ten people over the age of 18 whom you know and would like to ask a few questions.

2. Approach each of these people and ask each of them this question: "If you could go back in time, what do you wish you knew about money when you were 18 that you didn't?" (Feel free to have a long conversation if you like, and feel free to discuss related topics like anything that involves money, like college, cars, savings, investments, credit cards, relationships—well anything.)

3. Bonus points if this person gives you a job, helps you apply for a college scholarship, gets you started on investing, or otherwise helps you begin a strong financial life.

Format

* Concise Bullet Points are okay. For example:

Lacey → I wish I would have understood how overwhelmingly important relationships are. I would have written the five people I knew with the highest FQ (Financial Intelligence Quotient) and spent time with them every week or two for five years, asked them questions actively, and tried what they suggested.

Macey → I wish I would have opened up a Roth IRA when I was 18.

Have you seen the tables of what happens when you start investing at 18 vs. 26? The difference is about $1,000,000!

Tracey → I wish I would have done a monthly budget starting at age 16 (or 12), and I wish I would have read more about personal finance, including what the Bible says.

Extra Credit Alternative Format

* If you love to interview and/or write, I give you permission to interview someone at length, and to write in the format of your choice. Essay? Narrative style? Bullet points with pictures? Some of the above? Something else? It's up to you.

Ages 23 to 29

Envision Your Life

Part One: Life #1 → Future You

1. Write 3 to 20 paragraphs (200 to 3,000 words) envisioning your life from ages 23-29.

Are you married?

Do you have kids?

Did you go to college?

Graduate school?

Did you travel to Europe, Australia, Mexico? Thailand?

What work do you do?

How many hours a week do you work?

What is your annual salary?

What does your spouse (if you are married) do?

What kind of recreation do you enjoy?

What are your hobbies?

What do you read, study, or learn?

What attention (if any) do you pay to your nutrition, exercise, sleep, and stress-level habits?

What do you invest in?

What else do you envision?

* * Read **Part Three** before you start. * *

* * * Really get into it. If you are a poor writer and/or don't like to write, talk it out first with a friend and then write it. * * *

2. Do you plan to go to college? Where is your *best guess* as to where you will go to college? (Do not say, "I don't know.")

3. Cost?

4. Degree(s)?

5. Employment and/or Career Path when finished?

6. Did you give serious, thoughtful, in depth answers to all five questions? If not, go back and fix these.

Part Two: The Three Ghosts of Christmas Future

Instructions: Write about all three scenarios.

One) Graduation with $70,000 or more in student loans.

Write 200 to 3,000 words on what this does to your plans.

Two) Graduation without Debt

Write 200 to 500 words as to how you can make this happen.

Three) Graduate with Several Major Assets.

Explanation from my friends, Jim, Matt, Bryan, and Michael.

* Jim urges us to "get on the other side" where people pay you interest instead of you paying them interest.

* Matt's business partner, Ryan always lived without debt, and now Breakout KC, Breakout Waikiki, and the other Breakouts did $20,000,000 in sales last year.

* Bryan bought his first house at age 21. Other people (roommates) got a sweet deal on rent and he paid nothing for the house. In fact, he pocketed a few hundred dollars a month from it! And picked up a lot of skills in owning it, like how to get broken things fixed, and the people skills it takes to choose reliable roommates, and to tease rent out of them.

* Michael bought his first house at 24. Now he has six houses. When they are all paid for, they will be worth (IDK) $400,000 to $900,000. Like Bryan, he gave his roommates a generous deal on rent, and he paid nothing for the house.

* Here are the best investments in life:

+ Houses and land.

+ Index funds—because they outperform 99.9% of all mutual funds, stocks, and bonds.

+ Business experience outside of the college classroom.

+ No debt; emergency fund.

+ Five accomplished friends: you are the average of the five people you spend the most time with.

+ A sharp mind.

+ A personal mission in life.

+ EQ, Negotiation, and Leadership Skills

Instructions:

1) List three major assets you could graduate from college with.

2) Explain how you could acquire each.

3) Who could help you?

Part Three: Life #1 → Personal Mission vs. Career vs. Job

Explanation: A person can have a Personal Mission, a Career, or a J.O.B. (Just over Broke.) The most satisfied people who make the most money appear to have a Personal Mission.

Instructions: As a separate paper—maybe about 40 to 4,000 words long—explain your Personal Mission to me.

Your PM may have anywhere from one to ten aspects. For example, mine has three.

* Be specific, and explain how your PM creates your:

a) Career choices.

b) Savings, debt, budgeting, and investing decisions.

c) Social and emotional life?

d) Faith life.

Part Four: Life #2 →

Explanation: Since 1969, the d.school of Stanford University has a class for "Designing Your Life." To get people unstuck, and thinking more creatively, and thinking like a designer, they have people devise three separate lives for themselves.

Instructions: Maybe you did Life #1 for 12 years. Or maybe you changed your mind about it when you were 19, and it never happened. So, on a separate paper—maybe about 250 to 4,000 words long, write an essay explaining what Life #2 for you would look like.

Part Five: Life #3 →

Instructions: Same instructions as for Life #2. What is Life #3? Write about 125 to 4,000 words about this version of your future life.

For Life #1, Life #2, and Life #3, Strongly Consider →

Instructions: Given where we live, who our parents are, and where we go to school, this may be thinking *very differently*, but recall:

* Podcast #1: Faster + Cheaper Alternatives to College (*Art of*

Manliness #449)

* Podcast #2: The Case for Blue Collar Work with Mike Rowe (*Art of Manliness* #308)

And **consider**:

a) Use a search engine and look up "10 High-Paying Blue Collar Jobs 2018"

b) Look into "Last Mile" Programs

c) Look into Income Shares (that's where you pay nothing; the school helps you get a job; then you pay).

d) Look into employer pays

Related:

Could you become someone's apprentice?

The Art of Manliness Podcast Exploration

Exploring Both Shorter College Programs

and Blue Collar Careers

Because college is now more high stakes than ever before, it's helpful to consider alternatives. Remember: if you make money now instead of going to college, it may actually be easier to handle college later **(Part IV: College without Debt)**.

Instructions

1. Please listen to one or both of these podcasts at the links provided. Also available on iTunes, Stitcher, Spotify, Castbox, and Sound Cloud.

2. Exercise: Write 500 words. a) Summarize, b) Say what you thought; and c) Can this apply to you?

Option 1: Faster & Cheaper Alternatives to College
https://www.artofmanliness.com/articles/podcast-449-faster-and-cheaper-alternatives-to-college/

Option 2: Understand the skills deficit in order to make a lot of money
https://www.artofmanliness.com/articles/mike-rowe-interview/

The creator of the *Art of Manliness* podcast, Brett McKay, is an incredible man who does a lot of good in the world. Further, he has a summary of this podcast available at the two links listed above.

The Best Way to Shop

I. Pile-SPACE with Friends

II. Decide What You Need

III. Go with the Top People and/or *Consumer Reports*

I. Pile-SPACE with Friends

Before I define Pile-SPACE, a great idea from Julie Morgenstern, who wrote *Organize from the Inside Out*, let me point out that it makes use of a great fact of life, the 80/20 Principle.

Which is what?

Discovered by a 19th Century Italian Economist, Villfredo Pareto, the 80/20 Principle points out that 20% of your efforts give you 80% of your results...

...and 80% of your efforts give you 20% of your results.

Sometimes, life is skewed even worse than that. It can be 90/10, 95/5, or even 99/1. For example:

* 20% of your friends give you 80% of your happiness.

* You probably wear 20% of your clothing 80% of the time.

* Your family uses 20% of your dishes repeatedly...for 80% of your meals & snacks.

* 2% of the people you know give you 95% of your frustration.

When "A" students figure out what 20% of their efforts give them

80% of their results, they can *stop doing* the other 80%. This frees up an enormous amount of time.

For example, maybe an A student knows that if they just read the book twice, outline it, and listen to their excellent instructor, that is all they need to do.

Or maybe completing a study guide and rereading it every day for a week will get them an A—*and* help them remember more six months later.

Businesses often find that 20% of their products provide 80% of their profits. Sometimes, they stop offering the other 80% of their products. Why bother?

A software company, 37signals, makes programs like Microsoft Word that only do four to six things. Microsoft Word does thousands of things, but who needs all that? 95% of the functions are just clutter, and they confuse people. Thus, 37signals is popular and profitable.

That's the 80/20 Principle. It's also called "The Rule of the Vital Few." And it works well with Pile-SPACE, explained here:

Pile

Take all of your clothes and spread them out in your room so that you can see everything.

(Do this with friends who have excellent clothing intelligence.)

S: Sort

Sort everything.

P: Purge

Purge everything that you will never use. It doesn't make any difference how "nice" it is. Sell, give, or throw it away.

A: Arrange

Arrange all similar items.

C: Containerize

Place them on shelves, in drawers, in appropriate containers, etc.

E: Equalize

Re-do this every six months.

II. Decide What You Need

Don't buy anything just yet. Instead, write down what you need. Five of these…two of those…ten of these…one of that….

When you've planned your attack, you can attack your plan.

Where to Shop? Used or New?

* Used is often 50 to 90% off.

* craigslist, eBay, and other sites

* Thrift Stores

* Kohls (and similar places)

How Much Money Do You Take?

192

Decide this in advance and bring only that.

How do you avoid impulse shopping?

* Anything that is an impulse buy gets the 24-hour wait period rule.

* Use *Fun vs. Happiness.* Can you get the same thing (or something better!) for cheaper?

But some people love to shop for entertainment

* Window shop. That's free.

* Ask: what would you rather have the money for? Money spent on clothing *can't be spent on something else.* For example, if you have a big enough emergency fund, you can always quit your job when it becomes agonizing.

But What If Clothes & Fashion Are Your #1 Passion or Hobby?

Go for it!! But only *if*:

* It fits into the larger context of your budget

* You have a sizeable Emergency Fund that covers 3 to 6 months of your expenses.

* You've already done Pile-SPACE. With Pile-SPACE, you *purge* all the junk before you

get anything new.

* You almost never buy anything that *only goes* with itself. Ideally, any item you buy

should go with about five other things. Five skirts & five shirts, for example, could create 25

separate outfits. (Add in five pairs of shoes and we're up to 125.)

I believe 100% that you should get the item you truly want, and not a substitute. You'll never wear or use the substitute, you won't like it, and even if it was $1, that makes it a waste of time and money.

Ideally, you should only own things that *bring you joy*, as Marie Kondo says in her gem, *The Life-Changing Magic of Tidying Up*. If clothing/fashion are your #1 thing—and not #2—then I'd save up and go for it even if everyone around you says that it's too expensive.

III. Go with the Top People

Only take advice from, and only shop with, the *best* people. That is, the top 10%. You wouldn't take advice for how to make an "A" from someone with a 71% GPA. They might be your best friend, and a great person, but for the most part, they can't tell you what you need to know.

Sometimes, the people who are the best at something have no ability to explain it. But you can still learn from them by observation.

Budget Case Study

Note: The case study comes after these eight questions; you can use the experience of doing that to help you write a budget for yourself.

Assignment

1) Make a budget for yourself.

2) It may help to look at someone else's budget—a girl named Abby—and follow the eight steps listed below to help her.

Please make your budget easier to read. Instructions:

1. Income:

Include a **Total.** This number must match the total in Expenses.

2. Expenses:

a) Include a **Total.** This number must match the total in Income.

b) Savings is listed under expenses. I know that sounds weird to some people, but that's how it's done. The reason? Because you're supposed to "pay yourself first," and commit to saving before you spend anything on anyone else.

3. **Opportunity Cost:** Multiply each item in your budget by 64. Why? Because every dollar now, if invested in a Vanguard index fund, could double every 7.5 years. That means that in 45 years, $1 today = $64 in the future!

Note: How old will you be in 52.5 years? 68, 69, or 70? If you'd rather calculate things for 52.5 years from now, *multiply each item by 128.*

4. Do *Fun vs. Happiness* for every expense.

Next to each expense, write down an alternative that would be both:

a) cheaper/free; and

b) more fun.

5. List some Things to Sell.

List things around the house that you don't like or need.

* * * Note: Offer to put these items on eBay or craiglist. Or perhaps take them to a thrift store, or hold a garage sale! * * *

6. List some at least two other ways you could raise cash.

List at least two.

7. What are your long-term (meaning within the next 1 to 6 months) goals?

Also, please understand that "be a millionaire," is only a goal if you have a specific plan that comes with it. Otherwise, it's a dream. Dreams are good; however, I'm asking for **goals** (which have plans attached).

8. Annoying Expenses.

List at least one way you spend money that you wish you didn't, and propose a solution *that does not only rely on willpower.* Example: Don't say, "I could avoid spending money on food by not eating." Instead say, "I could: a) bring extra food that I like so I'm not tempted to eat expensive, unhealthy food, and b) I could leave all of my money at home."

The idea is to use creative intelligence first and willpower (if at all) second.

(This idea comes from the book *Atomic Habits*, which is all about getting just 1% better each day until you are unstoppable. The two most effective ways of changing your habits are to:

a) Change your identity

b) Change your environment.

9. For this month, ***write down all of your spending.   We are now keeping track.***

*   *   *

It may help to look at someone else's budgets, and help her make cuts.

Abby, 16

Help a Great Girl with Her Budget

MONTHLY INCOME

745 Job

25   Parents

GRAND TOTAL INCOME

770 Total

MONTHLY EXPENSES

* * * **Charity**

10.00   Starving Zimbabwe Orphan

20.50   Local church

* * * **Savings**

22.50

* * * **Taxes**

90.00

* * * Food

30.00   Groceries

50.00   Convenience Stores

50.00   Fast Food

* * * Car

50.00   Gas

33.00   Insurance

* * * Cell Phone

50.00

* * * Fun

13.00   Amazon Prime

10.00   Spotify

10.00   Ballgames

30.00   Movies

40.00   Pizza

50.00   Videogames

20.00   Bowling

23.00   Dates

* * * Health & Looks

45.00   Gym membership

33.00   Makeup

20.00   Hair

* * * Long-Term Expenses

50.00   Clothes

20.00   Christmas

GRAND TOTAL EXPENSES (Is her math right?)

770.00

3. OPPORTUNITY COST

(Abby forgot to do this)

4. FUN VS. HAPPINESS FOR EACH EXPENSE

(Abby forgot to do this)

5. THINGS TO SELL

(nothing listed)

6. TWO ADDITIONAL WAYS TO RAISE CASH

(nothing listed)

7. LONG-TERM GOALS

(nothing listed)

8. SOMETIMES, ABBY ANNOYS HERSELF

After a long day, Abby sometimes stops at McDonald's and—in her mind—wastes anywhere from $3 to $15. Later, she kicks herself, and thinks that was a waste of time, money, and calories.

What suggestions would you make for Abby to stop doing this? Other than, "Stop doing this?"

Alternative #1:

Alternative #2:

Career Exploration

When you are 23 to 26 (or 23 to elderly, if you like) and ask yourself these questions:

1. Am I more of a math & science person, an English person, a social studies person, an athletic and sporty person, a business-minded person, or something else?

2. Do I want to work for someone else, be my own boss, or do some of both?

3. How do I feel about debt?

4. Some jobs require that you work an average amount; some can be 10-12 hours a day. About how many hours a day do you want to work?

5. How do you feel about working nights?

6. Weekends?

7. How much do you want to get paid per year?

8. Do you want to be in a job where you get to argue a lot (like lawyer, or police officer, or perhaps administrator), or do you want a mostly friendly, everybody-gets-along workplace? (America needs both people who argue, like lawyers, and people who work in cooperative businesses.)

In other words, do you prefer *confrontation* or cooperation (each is about 50% of the population).

9. What age group do you want to be around?

10. Do you want to work by yourself or with a team?

11. Do you want a career where you might have to go back to school and pick up a few extra classes?

12. How many years of school are you willing to do?

What Questions Should I Have Asked?

12.

13.

14.

Exploration

1. Make a list of seven things you once loved to do as a kid. (Take your previous list if you like.)

a)

b)

c)

d)

e)

f)

g)

2 to 8. Now translate each of those into a potential career.

For example: in childhood, loved playing with Legos. Career: construction, engineering, architect, NASA, computer programming, IT, building, designing, creating, and much, much more.

2.

3.

4.

5.

6.

7.

8.

9 to 13. Now go online and find a personality test—maybe https://www.16personalities.com/free-personality-test--but there are lots of MBTI tests.

After you take one, look at the suggested careers. Write five down.

9.

10.

11.

12.

13.

14 to 18. Now list five careers that—if you had to—you would be willing to investigate *this week.*

14.

15.

16.

17.

18.

19 to 23. Now list three people you know who work in each of these

careers.

19.

20.

21.

22.

23.

24. When it comes to personal missions, careers, family, and more, no one is happy all the time; no one is 100% confident this is where they should be; and sometimes, it's difficult, even impossible. Are you prepared to suck it up, Buttercup?

25. What could you do in life that would strengthen your self-discipline?

a)

b)

c)

26 to 28. Want to have a happy, meaningful life? Try these question:

26. What's your purpose?

27. If you could only accomplish one major career activity in life, what would it be?

28. If were a billionaire and had all the time in the world, to what cause or causes would you dedicate millions of dollars and possibly thousands of hours of your life?

29 to 31. The Rocking Chair Test. You are 103 years old, in good health, and mentally sharp. You are on the porch surrounded by family and friends. You love to tell stories, and they have gathered to hear you tell about your amazing life.

What do you have to say?

Final Note: Consider either *interviewing* or *job shadowing* all three, and writing a paper about these experiences.

Cars

Four Ways to Buy

1. Millionaire Method #1 (from *The Millionaire Next Door*, by Dr. Thomas Stanley)

2. Millionaire Method #2 (from *The Millionaire Next Door*, by Dr. Thomas Stanley)

3. How Most Americans Buy Cars

4. When You Need a Car Today

5. The History of Car Buying, and Who Is Out of Date

6. Added Complexity

7. Car Repairs

1. Millionaire Method #1: Select a Car Dealer Who Is 100% Honest

Dr. Thomas Stanley is Dave Ramsey's mentor and a professor of economics. Over a fifty year career, he has extensively surveyed over 1,500 millionaires, often repeatedly. People who *grew up poor or middle class* and later *became millionaires* tend to buy cars in one of two ways.

These millionaires, incidentally, ended up with about $1,000,000 to $3,000,000 by retirement. The top 1% of Americans often follow similar methods. (See his book *The Millionaire Mind*, which is about the top 1%.)

Method #1: Even when poor or middle class, roughly 50% of the future millionaires *did no research about cars whatsoever* because they are very busy, and/or have no interest in learning about cars. Instead, they researched car dealers, chose one they could trust, told the dealer exactly what they were looking for, and let the dealer spend 2 to 4 weeks finding a car for them.

a) Make a list of 3 to 5 persons (dealers) you trust 100%.

b) If you don't trust someone 100%, *scratch this dealer off your list.* You really only need one.

c) Also, is your dealer thinking of you as a long-term customer? Let the dealer know you want to work together for the next twenty years, that you'd like to be a loyal customer, and that you'll recommend the dealer's business to all your friends. If your dealer is not a long-term partner, *scratch this dealer off the list.*

d) Now make a list of qualities you'd like in a car.

e) But think like a future millionaire. In other words, you are poor or middle class right now, but you will have $100,000 to $1,000,0000 in the bank *and no debt* when you are 29 years old. You didn't win the lottery. You earned money slowly and saved incrementally. Which means you didn't load the car up with expensive extras.

f) Did you list *extremely well-made; low maintenance; easy to repair; lasts forever?* If not, add those in.

g) Did you list *12 to 24 months old?* If not, add that in. Here's how you know the used car is reliable: you trust the dealer 100%.

h) Remove anything from the list that is expensive and unnecessary (like sunroofs, which can add hundreds to the bill).

Final note.

Future millionaires think, "There is nothing wrong with buying the most expensive car in the world *if you can pay for 100% of it in cash.*" If you have the cash—and your college & house are completely paid for, and you have no debts of any kind—get the $50,000 car.

2. Millionaire Method #2: Do Your Own Research

Dr. Thomas Stanley (see above biography) surveyed over 1,500 millionaires, often repeatedly, and learned that *even when poor or middle class*, roughly 50% did their own research for cars, and then shopped around.

a) Before leaving the house, people who were poor or middle class at first and millionaires later made a list on paper of qualities they'd like in a car. Please do that now.

b) Did you list *extremely well-made; low maintenance; easy to repair; lasts forever?* If not, add those in.

c) Did you list *12 to 24 months old?* If not, add that in.

d) What fun things like "sunroof" did you list that you can *scratch off?* Fun things can cost hundreds of dollars. Comfort and convenience = easy money for car sellers to take from you.

e) Now Google "What cars last the longest?" and "Most reliable kinds of cars." Write down three to five brands that you find acceptable.

f) Do comparison/contrast. Make tables with rows & columns; look at *Kelly's Blue Book* and *Consumer Reports* or similar publications. Start analyzing price, features, etc.

g) You are almost ready to go shopping. You *definitely* want a car that is 12 to 18 months old and off of this list. But where to do?

h) Buy from an individual and *pay in cash.* Look on craigslist, eBay, etc.

i) Go to a dealer that your friends recommend as 100% honest and tell him or her what you want.

j) Post on social media and elsewhere what you are looking for.

You are well on your way! But see **Part VI: Added Complexity.**

3. How Most Americans Buy Cars

When I Googled "What percentage of Americans have car payments," all of the top hits said Americans are borrowing more than ever, and that car payments are now our #1 financial priority. That's debatable (what about student loans?), but let's sign up for car payments.

Scenario A: So, let's get a fully loaded SUV for $34,000. That's fairly average.

a) How much is a $34,000 SUV? Go to

http://www.bankrate.com/calculators/auto/auto-loan-calculator.aspx or any online calculator and find out.

b) What is your monthly payment? (You choose.)

c) For how many months? (You choose.)

d) How much interest did you pay?

e) What did you pay altogether? Principle + Interest = ?

f) Wait, you aren't done. Let's say you pay 25% in Federal income tax. That means your total tax bill (Federal + FICA + Medicare + Kansas + Sales Tax + Property Tax) is probably closer to 40%. So, multiply "e" by 1.40 to see how much you actually had to earn to buy this $34,000 car. What do you get?

Scenario B: Choose Your Own Brand of Car

1. What kind?

2. Go to http://www.bankrate.com/calculators/auto/auto-loan-calculator.aspx

3) What is your monthly payment? (You choose.)

4) For how many months? (You choose.)

5) How much interest did you pay?

6) What did you pay altogether? Principle + Interest = ?

7) The real cost: you are paying 25% in Federal Income Tax. That means your total tax bill (Federal + FICA + Medicare + Kansas + Sales Tax + Property Tax) is probably closer to 40%. So, multiply "e" by 1.40 to see how much you actually had to earn to buy this $34,000 car.

4. When You Need a Car Today

People buy cars out of desperation every day in America. While some are lucky, here is the best math I can think of:

a) Go to **Part III: How Most Americans** and do all of the math for Scenario A.

b) And Scenario B.

c) Multiply the total in Scenario A by 1.5 or even 2.

d) Multiply the total in Scenario B by 1.5 or even 2.

5. The History of Car Buying, and Who Is Out of Date

A writer about neuroscience and business, popular author/podcaster Daniel Pink wrote *To Sell Is Human*, and has a long chapter on car sales that appears accurate to me. He points out that places like CarMax represent the future, while your old-fashioned dealers, while still a huge portion of the market, represent the past.

In the modern market, car buyers are very cynical about car dealers. They think most of them are crooks. They hate buying cars because buying cars usually involves:

* Asymmetrical information: the dealer knows a lot, and s/he is withholding that information.

* Negotiation, and at least half the population hates to negotiate. They hate it for many reasons, including the fact that they think the dealer is

lying to them, but they don't know when, where, or about what.

* It's easy to make an expensive mistake.

* Emotion and feature-*itis* takes over and logic gets tossed out the window.

* Cars come with too much emotional baggage. They are status symbols for many. On some level, many people are concerned with how other people perceive them. On some level, buyers know they sometimes make decisions they know aren't good for them because they feel the need to please other people, who—ironically—don't really care.

* Deep down, we know that this hunk of metal will break down too fast, get dented, cost too much in repairs, and that the thrill will wear off in about a week.

But there's more. Specifically, about the money:

* We know we overpay.

* It's hard to negotiate unless you pay in cash because you start from a disadvantage.

* They play games with the financing, and the bottom line.

So, the new way has come along, because the car buying/selling business is ripe for disruption, just as taxis got disrupted by Uber and horse-and-buggies got disrupted by cars. The new method is actually an old method. It's just that the Internet makes it easier.

The New Method

1. Decide what you want before you leave the house.

2. Comparison shop online.

3. *If* you visit a dealer—or buy a car off of craigslist, eBay, etc.—you walk in with a printout of all of the relevant information. (Price, mileage, longevity, ease of repairs, frequency of repairs, etc.)

4. You negotiate with these "Five Keys."

1. Win/win or No Deal. This means *both sides win 100% or you walk away*.

2. The person with the most information wins.

3. The person who *cares the least* has the most power.

4. Always act with the highest honesty & integrity.

5. You are in no hurry to buy anything. If it takes a month or two, that's even better.

As stated, smart shoppers have *always* comparison shopped, taken their time, and negotiated. It's just that you can do all of these things so much faster online.

6. Added Complexity

If we were playing a board game called *Easy Come, Easy Go*, we could have squares on the board that looked like this:

* You buy a new car. Thrilled about all the features and subconsciously hoping to look good among your social circle, you overpay by $8,000. *Move back ten squares.*

* You buy a new car. You ask, "What's the monthly payment?" *Move back eight squares.*

* You buy a car that's 12 months old. You ask, "How much is the whole car?" *Move ahead ten squares.*

* You buy a car. The dealer tries to get you to add a sunroof, special seats, and the Latest Screens 2.0. That's an extra $4,000. *Move back five squares.*

* You don't like to negotiate, so you sign. That's an extra $6,000. *Move back seven squares.*

* You don't do any research other than asking your broke cousins who have cool cars what they do. *Move back nineteen squares and miss a turn.*

* You panic buy. *Roll three dice and move back that many squares.*

* Your job is *the worst,* but you can't quit because you & your spouse both need to work to pay off all your loans. You sign up for car payments. *Move back thirty squares or move back to square one; you choose.*

* Other than keeping your car clean, you are impervious to social trends, so you buy a used car for $5,000 because you've read up on that model, and you can probably get eight years out of it, and not have to put more than $1,000 in repairs into it. *Move ahead eighteen squares.*

* You finance the car. *Move back ten squares.*

* You pay in cash. *Move ahead twenty squares.*

* You don't pay more than ½ of what you are making annually on all of your vehicles put together. *Move ahead fifteen squares.*

* When you have over $100,000 in the bank + your college educations + your house are 100% paid for, you get any car you feel like. *Move ahead twenty-five squares.*

Points to Consider

* Most Americans are in debt.

* Most Americans have car payments.

* The average car payment is at least $475 per month, but that's more like $633-$750 after taxes. (Given a tax rate of 25%, + FICA + Medicare + Kansas + Sales Tax + Property Tax.)

* Most Americans can't quit their jobs even if they want to.

* We work hard to pay for things we don't truly enjoy all that much. We just think we must have them.

When You Avoid Car Payments, You Avoid:

* Buying cars in a hurry. See **Part IV. When You Need a Car Today**

* All the games the car finance people play—games rigged against you.

* Many of the agonies of negotiation.

* That feeling that you're getting ripped off due to asymmetrical information.

Final Recommendations

* Don't look for the "one right car." Use the WRAP Framework to find *five* great options. Then choose.

* Google ""Which cars last the longest?" and "Most reliable kinds of cars."

* Use Method #1 or Method #2, the Millionaire Methods.

* Pay close attention to the cars others drive, and the circumstances surrounding those cars. You will see these ideas jump out at you. It's highly instructive.

7. Car Repairs

Two scenarios:

Make Repairs Unnecessary

* Do the regularly scheduled maintenance; change the oil every 3,000 miles; take the attitude that you will get this car past 200,000 or even 300,000 miles, which means it needs to go to the doctor (mechanic) all the time for *preventative* maintenance.

* Baby your car; keep it clean; spend money on preventative maintenance; this is like spending $100 on your health now and avoiding a

$250,000 medical bill later. "An ounce of prevention is worth a pound of cure." – Benjamin Franklin, Founding Father, scientist, author, genius, and philanthropist.

When Forced to Repair

* Fix it yourself, or have family fix it. Most people have a cousin or a close friend (or friend of a friend) who loves fixing cars. Ask around today; don't wait until it's broken.

* Your genius neighbor whom you trust fixes your and *becomes your regular mechanic.*

* Your dealer that *you trust 100%* fixes it every time, and knows your car like he knows his family.

* Before you take it to any shop that you don't know, you've exhausted all of the above. You've asked around three or four times.

* If forced to go to the shop, have them look it over and *don't get it fixed.* Take your car out of that shop; take it to a new shop and get a second opinion. *Maybe* get it fixed, but:

* Fix as little of the car as possible. Just get your car roadworthy, unless the repairs are under $100.

* If your car has a lot of miles on it, like over 70,000, you may want to avoid getting anything fixed that is nonessential.

* The instant you buy a new-to-you car, start saving immediately for the car after that. The bigger this car emergency fund is, the longer your current car will last.

College and WRAP

Use the Best Decision-Making Model to Choose Your College Life

Introduction

This exercise will test your ability to bring many Personal Finance concepts like negotiation, getting a promotion, and living out a personal mission together, and it will test your ability to think, and express yourself clearly.

A New Decision Making Model

In the United States, there are only three very common *methodologies* of making decisions:

* Praying about it.

* Making "Pros vs. Cons" lists.

* Asking and/or reading for advice.

* Ruminating about it (perhaps endlessly) and in the end, going with your intuition.

* Not thinking about it: acting impulsively.

According to university business and psychology professors, most of these methods either come with massive pitfalls, or they are fatally flawed.

* The Pros & Cons method suffers from Confirmation Bias.

* Asking for advice is good—if you're asking the right person who *fully understands* your situation!

* Ruminating: People spin their wheels endlessly *with incomplete*

information. We cannot predict the future. A study of political pundits found out that when making predictions, the best pundit was wrong 91% of the time (*Decisive*, Dan & Chip Heath).

* Praying about it: God is not going to tell you the future. (Revelation 22:15.) I will elaborate in class. In fact, many spiritual directors say things like, "There are a thousand things you could do that would make God very happy." Decisions about matters like which college to attend concern God primarily in terms of what they will do to your love of God, and your ethics.

* Not thinking about it: self-explanatory.

What Should We Do Instead?

Use WRAP (see next sheet).

* Instead of "narrow framing," which engages in "whether or not thinking," we should **Widen Our Options**. The ideal number is 5 to 6; it avoids the paradox of choice. (More than 7 options tends to paralyze people.)

* To **Reality Test Your Assumptions** means to test things out. How can you do this in a small, less risky way before making a gigantic commitment?

* To **Attain Distance Before Deciding** means to sleep on it and get good counsel.

* **Prepare to be Wrong** is something almost no one does—except for billionaires like Richard Branson (net worth: $5,100,000,000), who founded over 400 companies. He says he always "protects the downside." In other words, he has an exit strategy in case things go wrong.

* **Set a Tripwire**. In real life, when someone stumbles over a tripwire, alarms go off. In this plan, it's good to set a tripwire. For example, a person might sell a stock if it falls in value by 30%, or they might stop

eating donuts for a month if they ever find themselves eating three at a time.

Exercise: Your College Major

After much thought, you've chosen a college major. (What is it?) Everything about this decision has been difficult. (Where will you attend? How much will a year cost? How many years will college take?) Even now, you are not 100% sure. After all, what if you don't love it? What if the professors are harder than expected? What if your field is over-crowded, and its hard to get a job? How will you stand out? What are you doing to be in the top 20% (zig)? And what are you doing to become invaluable (zag?)

Write a 200+ word essay that answers *__all ten questions__* above.

1a. **Widen Your Options**: What **5 or 6** options for college are you currently considering?

1b. **Reality Test Your Assumptions:** How could you test **each** of the above options before you spend tuition money?

1c. **Attain Distance Before Deciding:** Which **5 or 6** people could you interview (or discuss your ideas with) to make sure you are fully informed?

1d. **Prepare to be Wrong:** After a semester of college, it is going to be one of these four things:

> i. *Better* than what you expected.

> ii. *Worse* than you anticipated.

> iii. *Similar to* your expectations.

> iv. *Different* than you imagined.

Write at two sentences as to what you'll do in **each** circumstance.

1e. **Set a Tripwire**: What would make you say, "That's enough of that," and either switch your major or leave your college? **Why?**

Credit Card Inferno vs. Investment Paradiso

1. Your friends Lacey, Tracy, Macy, Stacy, Pacey, and Fifi Trixibelle all get credit cards. Average balance after college: $10,000. Average interest rate: 18%. What are your initial thoughts about this?

2. Use an amortization calculator online to see how long it will take each friend to pay off her debt.

Either use a search engine to find an amortization calculator, or perhaps use:

https://smartasset.com/credit-cards/credit-card-calculator#HtbmAp2DRk

https://www.daveramsey.com/blog/investment-calculator/#/entry_form

http://www.bankrate.com/calculators/savings/compound-savings-calculator-tool.aspx

3. Let's pay $200 per month because that's typical. How many months does it take to pay off the debt?

4. What was the interest?

5. What was the principal (also called "starting amount")?

6. How much did you pay altogether?

7. Circle one:

    a) Paying all this money for this long sucks.

    b) This is life. Let's not make a big deal out of it. It's a big crap sandwich; let's eat it.

    c) What a great situation!

New Story

9. Your friend Sophia, 18, does *not* take out a credit card. Instead, she takes $1,000 and invests it in VFINX, VDAIX, or VTSMX or another index fund that averages 9.5% return—at least, that's what the market has done since at least 1895. *And* she adds another $83.33 per month—every month.

    (In other words, an 18-year-old invests $1,000 to start and $83.33 per month at a growth rate of 9.5%.)

10. How much does she have in 5 years?

11. 10 years?

12. 20 years?

13. After college, Sophia gets a job that pays between $50,000 and $100,000. If you were her, would you start putting a lot more than $83.33 per month? Why?

14 to 16. Let's discuss quality of life issues. List three possible facts that your friends, Lacey, Tracy, Macy, Stacy, Pacey, and Fifi Trixibelle may have to cope with between ages 20 to 30.

14.

15.

16.

17 to 19. What potential opportunities might your friends, Fifi Trixibelle, Spacy, and the rest—have to pass up?

17.

18.

19.

20. Your friends, Brad, Chad, Tad, and Vlad the Impaler also all get credit cards. (Vlad usually taps into other people's blood, but he's got nothing on the credit card companies.) Average balance after college: $9,000. Average interest rate: 19.4%. Each pays $180 per month.

Q. How long does it take to pay off the debt?

21. How much interest does that come to?

22. What was the principal?

23. What is the total amount paid?

24. Choose one:

a) That's a long time to pay off a gigantic amount of money. It will cut into the ability of these men to invest and build wealth.

b) That's life.

c) What a bargain!!

25. Your friend Axel does not take out a credit card. Instead, he invests $7,000 by the time he is 22 in an eTrade index fund. It grows at 9.5%. Further, he adds $1,000 every month after that. How much does he have when he is 25?

26. Axel, age 30.

27. Axel, age 40.

28. Axel, age 80, when he's in great shape and plays a lot of tennis on his private island.

29 to 31. Let's discuss quality of life issues. List three possible facts that your friends, Axel and Sophia may enjoy between ages 20 to 33.

29.

30.

31.

32 to 34. What potential opportunities might your friends, Sophia & Axel—who end up getting married, and having seven children—enjoy?

32.

33

34.

35. Extra Credit: What are the names of Axel & Sophia's seven children?

Fun vs. Happiness, Part I

Chasing Down Fun Is Often No Fun, and Expensive

Premise

Often, we spend money in a weak effort to *have fun* or *buy someone else's friendship*—and we find out it doesn't work. We have very little fun, we feel like we've wasted our time, and the other person doesn't like us any more than when we started.

Assignment

1. Make three columns on a blank sheet of paper:

a) ACTIVITY YOU'VE DONE or ITEM YOU BOUGHT IN AN EFFORT TO HAVE FUN.

b) WHAT WERE YOU REALLY TRYING TO ACHIEVE?

c) HOW COULD YOU HAVE GOTTEN THE SAME THING EITHER CHEAPER OR FOR FREE?

2. List twelve activities or items you buy under the first column.

3. Complete the second and third column.

Example One.

Activity: You eat out with friends and spend $14. The food: average.

Goal: Have fun with friends; laugh; tell stories; drink water. Or spend $1.50 on tea. Enjoy your friends!

Cheaper/Free More Fun Alternative: Eat first, and then go out and deepen your friendships.

Example Two.

Activity: Go out to the movies with seven friends. Tickets: $7 each. Popcorn, etc: $7. Your total: $14, plus gas. But the movie was average or bad. Altogether, *everyone* spent $98, plus gas.

Goal: See great movie with friends.

Cheaper/Free More Fun Alternative: Invite friends over. RedBox: $1, plus gas. Super comfortable at home. Movie: Awesome, because you know it's reputation. Food: cheaper or free.

Fun vs. Happiness, Part II

Create Budget Alternatives So You Can

Increase Your Happiness While Keeping Your Money

Goals

1. Can you get the same thing for cheaper or free?

2. Can you get something *even better* for cheaper or free?

For example, would you rather pay $7 for a terrible movie at the theatre, or invite 7-12 friends over for a great time and maybe watch a RedBox hit for $1?

Inspirational Reminder

When you were five years old, you were creative. The marketplace rewards creativity with extra money for you. The problem with many adults is that they can only think of one thing to do. Recover your creativity while your brain is still flexible.

What You Must Do

1. List 15 areas of life where you spend money. Feel free to use any of these:

Tithe

Savings

Saving for College

Debt Reduction

Groceries

Gas

Phone

Random food

Dining out

Games

Sports

Music

Hair

Cosmetics

Toiletries

Entertainment

Concerts

Christmas

Birthdays

Clothing

Vacation

New electronic item

2. Put down how much you spend on each.

3. List the *motive* for what you spend on each item.

4. For each item, list three places you could go *instead* to get the *same thing* or *something better* for a lot cheaper, or even free!

5. Take a recent decision you made (such as buying an iPod, or going to the game) and write about it using the WRAP framework.

Renter, Owner, and/or Landlord?

Who Will Win?

Answering these questions takes 30-90 minutes, and will be eye-popping in terms of what the best, average, and worst living situations are. Many people really don't think too hard about this, but a house is the most expensive thing most people will ever buy. Let's save a lot of heartache and tens of thousands of wasted dollars spent on interest—not to mention all the time you have to work in order to pay that interest.

Btw, I used simple numbers to make it easier, but they are realistic. You can always double everything or cut it all in half, depending on where you live.

Preliminary Thoughts: Let's consider these six options:

+ Rent with friends.

+ Buy a house with a 30-year mortgage.

+ Rent by yourself.

+ Buy a house and get roommates you like to pay some/all of the expenses.

+ Buy a house with a 15-year mortgage.

+ The option you'd like that I didn't mention.

1. From *best* to *worst, list* each option in order of your personal preference for your life in college.

a.

b.

c.

d.

e.

f.

Why?

2. List each in order of your personal preference for your life at around ages 22-25.

a.

b.

c.

d.

e.

f.

Why?

Scenario One: 30-Year Mortgage

A Bad Deal?

You buy a house for $125,000 and make a 20% down payment, which means you still owe $100,000.

Note: If you select a house that is twice this much, then just double all of your final answers. Ditto if you choose a house that is three, four, or five times as expensive.

Monthly payment: $536

Insurance per month: $83

Property taxes: $167

Termite protection: $26

Gas, water, electric, and internet: $220 per month on average. (Gas is high in the winter but low in the summer; electricity is the reverse.)

a) Total for each month. _____

(P.S. Dave Ramsey says middle class people say, "How much is my monthly payment?" Meanwhile, wealthy people say, "What's the total bill?" The difference is short-term vs. long-term thinking.)

b) Total for the 30 years. _____

c) How much was the principle? (Hint: look above.)
_____

d) How much was the interest? (Subtract $100,000 from "b.")
_____

e) Is the number from "d" huge? _____

f) People feel like interest is money thrown in the trash. List three actions or emotions a person would feel if they realized just how much interest they are paying.

(P.S. It's not the money you pay that is frustrating. It's all the hours you realize you have to spend working in order to pay the money for interest.)

i)

ii)

iii)

g) Your friend is 15 years into paying her mortgage. She has $300 in savings. The economy now crashes like in 2008 and she loses her job and can't find a new one. She can't pay her mortgage. List three things she could do.

i)

ii)

iii)

* * * Note: People usually don't include utilities, repairs, and more when calculating expenses. That's a mistake. The things people leave out are the things that make their heads hurt later. If you have to pay it, you should include it.   * * *

Scenario Two: 15-Year Mortgage

The Winner? Or Second Place?

You buy a house for $125,000 and make a 20% down payment, which means you still owe $100,000.

Monthly payment: $791

Insurance per month: $83

Property taxes: $167

Termite protection: $26

Gas, water, electric, and internet: $220 per month on average. (Gas is high in the winter but low in the summer; electricity is the reverse.)

a) Total for each month. _____

b) Total for the 15 years. _____

c) How much was the principle? (Hint: look above.)
_____

d) How much was the interest? (Subtract $100,000 from "b.")
_____

e) Is the number from "d" huge? _____

f) Write down "d" from Scenario One, and also write down "d" from Scenario Two.

_____ *and* _____

g) Given how different these two numbers are, why do you think less than half of all home-owners put themselves on a 15-year mortgage?

h) Jot down any opinions you have about 30- vs. 15-year mortgages so far.

Scenario Three: Rent with Friends

More happiness for less money?

With some searching you and three friends rent a house (near the college?) for $1,000 per month. ($1,000 seems reasonable, but you should look up the neighborhood you're considering.)

Monthly payment: $300 (you take the big room)

Renter's insurance per month: $12

Property taxes: zero

Termite protection: zero

Your share of gas, water, electric, and internet: $100 per month on average.

a) What is your total per month? _____

b) What if you rent for 30 years? 33% of people in America rent. Some people always rent. How much is 30 years' worth of rent?
_____

c) How much did you save on insurance (compared to Scenario One or Two)? _____

d) How much did you save on property taxes? _____

e) How much did you save on termite protection?
_____

f) How much did you save total? _____

g) Jot down any opinions you have about renting vs. owning so far.

Scenario Four: Rent an Apartment

One-Bedroom Solitude

With some searching you find an apartment at 119th and Ridgeview in Olathe for $750 per month. (One kitchen area with a living room, one bedroom, & one bath.)

Monthly payment: $750 (you take the big room)

Renter's insurance per month: $12

Property taxes: zero

Termite protection: zero

Gas, water, electric, and internet: $95 per month on average.

a) What is your total per month? _____

b) What if you rent for 30 years? 33% of people in America rent. Some people always rent. How much is 30 years' worth of rent? _____

c) How much did you save on insurance (compared to Scenario One or Two)? _____

d) How much did you save on property taxes? _____

e) How much did you save on termite protection? _____

f) How much did you save total? _____

g) Jot down any opinions you have about renting vs. owning so far.

Scenario Five: Landlord

Never Pay Anything?

At age 19 like my friend, Bryan, or age 23-24 like my friend, Mike, you buy a house from Scenario Two: "15-Year Mortgage" for $125,000 and make a 20% down payment, which means you still owe $100,000.

Monthly payment: $791

Insurance per month: $83

Property taxes: $167

Termite protection: $26

Gas, water, and electric: $180 per month on average. (Gas is high in the winter but low in the summer; electricity is the reverse.)

a) What is your total per month? _____

b) Where you live, you can probably rent three or four spots out to people you like for an average of $425 each. Suppose you rent three. How much do you take in? _____

c) How much pocket each month? _____

d) Okay, so that's not much to pocket. What if you rented four spots for $375 each? How much do you pocket per month now? _____

e) Let's go per year. How much did you save on insurance per year (compared to Scenario One or Two)? _____

f) How much did you save on property taxes per year? _____

g) How much did you save on termite protection per year?

_____

h) How much did you save total on insurance, property taxes, and termite protection over the course of the year? (e + f + g = total.)

_____

i) Jot down any opinions you have about being a landlord.

j) Which of these skills do you think you could learn or do, or get help with?

_____Choosing reliable renters who will pay on time and not break things.

_____Having the people skills to share a house.

_____When things break, being able to fix them—or get someone in to fix them.

_____Keeping track of the money. (Who paid, how much, etc.)

_____Settling disputes.

_____If you made a mistake and rented to the wrong person, figuring out a good way to help that person move out.

k) If you bought a house early in life like Mr. Dorsey or Mr. Consiglio, who could give you advice and moral support?

    i)

    ii)

    iii)

l) What skills do you think you'd learn if you bought a house early?

    i)

ii)

iii)

Conclusions

What's best for you?

1. Under what circumstances would you rent?

2. Own?

3. Own, and rent to people whom you like?

4. Which of these, in your mind, is the best option?

5. Second best?

6. What would it take for the second best option to move up in the rankings?

Author's Note

Choosing where to live—if you have the option—is a deeply personal decision. That being said, I hope you realize that if we exclude all other considerations and just look at the money, then options, listed in order of best to worst, are as follows:

1. Landlord. You eliminate the mortgage, interest, taxes, and repair costs—and still get a house out of it. You can give your friends wonderfully cheap rent; they'll love you for it. You'll pick up dozens of leadership and management skills.

2. 15-Year Mortgage. *In a very short period of time, you own your house.*

3. Rent with friends in a house. *Very cheap; lots of space; possibly no lease; friendships grow; and you can learn how to be a landlord through observation.*

4. 30-Year Mortgage. *This is basically a half of a lifetime. At the end of it, you'll have paid well over twice as much interest compared to the* 15-Year Mortgage *scenario. The house really isn't yours. It's the bank's; you're taking care of it for them.*

5. Rent by yourself. *Horrifically expensive; tiny space; lots of restrictions imposed on you; and you leave with nothing.*

But don't take my word for it. Spend an hour calculating each option for yourself.

Start Your Own Business This Week

Brainstorm First, Then Select One Idea to Try

1a. Get an Idea. List 5 to 6 ideas from your childhood or your current passions here.

a)

b)

c)

d)

e)

Note: In The $100 Startup *and the podcast* Side Hustle School, *Chris Guillebeau points out that he loves pizza and videogames. However, no one will pay him to eat pizza or play videogames. So while it's fun to list your pleasures, please cross out unrealistic options.*

1b. List 5 to 6 Needs/Desires/Problems you see in the people around you.

a)

b)

c)

d)

e)

1c. Explain how 1 or 2 of these ideas from "1a" or "1b" could be turned into businesses.

a)

b)

2. Refine Your Idea. *Choose one idea.*

3. Make an Offer. How would you pitch this to a person face to face? Also, how would you post this on social media so as to get a response? (Answer both questions.)

4. Get the Word Out. List 3 methods you could employ.

a)

b)

c)

5. Learn as You Go and Fix It Later. Explain what three things you could do within the next 7 days.

a)

b)

c)

6a. Identify Helpers. List three.

a)

b)

c)

6b. Identify Mentors. List three.

a)

b)

c)

6c. Identify People You Could Help. (People you help might help you in return.) List three.

a)

b)

c)

7a. Spend $0 to $600. List what you need.

7b. Always Simplify. What is absolutely essential?

8. Work *on* Your Business. How will you keep track of income and expenses?

9a. **Common Objections.** List what the critics will say.

a)

b)

c)

9b. **Common Objections.** Refute the critics.

a)

b)

c)

d)

10. **Zig and Zag.**

a) Zig: What people or businesses are like you; who is your competition?

b) Zig: How are they like you?

c) Zag #1: How could you be the same but different; that is, what makes you first in your new category?

d) Zag #2

e) Zag #3

Start Your Own Business This Week

Choose One Idea and Go for It!

1. Refine Your Idea. *Choose one idea.*

2. Make an Offer. How would you pitch this to a person face to face? Also, how would you post this on social media so as to get a response? (Answer both questions.)

> *Look, you're probably going to have to:*
>
> *a) Make a flyer that can also be a PDF*
>
> *b) Write an email that others can pass along for you.*
>
> *c) Have a one or two sentence summary of what you do that you can recite to me. For example, "I will give you a dozen chocolate Paleo cupcakes for $2 each."*

4. Get the Word Out. List 4 methods you could employ.

a)

b)

c)

d)

6a. Identify Helpers. List three.

a)

b)

c)

6b. Identify Mentors. List three.

a)

b)

c)

6c. Identify People You Could Help. (People you help might help you in return.) List three.

a)

b)

c)

10. Reconfigure your Schedule So as to Make Time for Your Side Hustle. (We'll discuss this further.)

Time Management for Scholarships, Side Hustles, Art, or Big Projects

To Decide Is to Cut Away

Assignment: Create *three separate versions of your weekly or monthly (you choose) schedule.* You'll complete three schedules: see Plan A, B, and C below.

Bonus points: Do Plan Z.

* *Extra-Special Note*: The Key to This Assignment Is in Plan C. * *

Plan A: Either retrieve or write down your current schedule. (See reverse side for a possible model.)

Plan B: Now *free up* ten hours. Re-create your schedule to accommodate this.

Recommendation: Don't cut too much fun, or your self-discipline might collapse, and you won't get anything done.

Why are we doing this? To free up time to apply for scholarships.

Advice:

1) Do the essay scholarships—less competition.

2) Get two English majors, Journalism majors, or outstanding proofreaders to help you after you've done your essays so that they are a pleasure to read. (I've read people's scholarship applications. Some are delightful. Others are agonizing. Be delightful.

3) Tell the reader what you might do with your life, and how you plan to *make the community better.* They don't want to give you money

because you're so awesome. They want to give you money because you want to *give back*. That's what they think is 100% truly awesome.

Plan C: Now *free up* thirty hours.

If you had an emergency—if your favorite friend or cousin were deathly ill, and you were the only person who could be there—you would figure out a way to drop 50-100% of everything and just be with them.

Further, you would also do it in such a way that the essentials would not utterly fall apart.

Q #1. Which teachers, coaches, supervisors, and others would you need to communicate with so that they don't think you are a dropout?

Q #2. How could you "bottom line" or postpone each of these things for one month?

Plan Z: Eliminate areas of your life where you are *working against yourself*.

These could be little things, medium-sized things, or big things. Examples that involve either time or money:

Little things: Maybe you forget to bring a lunch to an event on a Saturday, and are forced to pay $15 for bad food.

Medium-sized thing: Maybe you never plan your time, and find yourself wasting five hours on screen time that sabotages your grades, sports, relationships, sleep, and life. You always scramble to get stuff done.

Big thing: Some people are addicted to cigarettes and smoke a pack a day. If a pack costs $5, that comes to $1,825 per year after taxes, which might the person has to earn $2,433- $2,725 at his job to get the cigarettes *and* taxes paid for. Plus, the person stains their clothes and teeth, has to stand outside when it's freezing, gets death stares from other people who hate cigarette smoke, and they get health problems starting at age 24.

WRAP Framework for Making Decisions

I discuss WRAP in **Part XIII: Make Better Decisions.** Please read that section. I bring this up because, ideally, *you are the one planning most of your schedule.* If you are, then congratulations: you're an adult!

Because adults have to make major decisions, I wanted to recap the best decision-making method that I know of, WRAP, below:

Widen Your Options → Think like a scientist, designer, or creative and come up with 5 to 6 good options. When you find the "right answer," then find the other right answer.

Reality Test Your Assumptions → Most people analyze, agonize, read, and talk about things before deciding. Forget that. Just sample the situation and then you'll have a lot more information. Stick your toe in the water; you don't need to jump in the pool.

Attain Distance Before Deciding → Sleep on it. Talk to a mentor. Don't make any decisions out of desperation or fear.

Prepare to Be Wrong → Almost nothing in life turns out the way people think. It's either a) better; b) worse; or just c) Different. So, plan in advance how you could get out of the situation just in case it is not to your liking.

Set a tripwire – This is an event or situation that helps you realize: I need to quit now.

Dreams, Goals, Bucket List for Next 6 to 12 Months

<u>Instructions</u>: List what—in an ideal world, if God removed all your obstacles—you'd do in the next 6 to 12 months.

A.

B.

C.

D.

E.

F.

G.

H.

Etc.

Plan A, Plan B, and Plan C.

Q. How Do You Spend Your Time? Briefly—don't get super-meticulous—sketch out how you spend your week.

* * * Recommended: Do all three on separate sheets of paper. * * *

	SUN.	MON.	TUES.	WED.	THURS.	FRI.	SAT.
5							
6							
7							
8							
9							
10							
11							
12							
1							
2							
3							
4							
5							
6							
7							
8							
9							
10							

Time Management Reality Check

1. Dreams, Goals, Bucket List for the Near Future (Meaning the next 1-12 months.)

A.

B.

C.

D.

E.

2. How Do You Spend Your Time? Briefly—*don't get super-meticulous*—sketch out how you spend your week.

SUNDAY		MONDAY		TUESDAY
WED.	THURSDAY		FRIDAY	SATURDAY

5

6

7

8

9

10

11

12

1

2

3

4

5

6

7

8

9

10

11

12

3. By the Hours: How You Spend Your Time

_____ Sleep

_____ Eating, Bathing, Getting Ready, That Kind of Thing

_____ School Day

_____ Homework

_____ Sport(s)

_____ Activity #1, 2, 3, etc. (Like sports, theatre, music, clubs, etc.)

_____ Job

_____ Social Life

_____ Other #1

_____ Other #2

_____ Other #3

_____ Other #4

_____ Other #5

_____ Misc.

_____ TOTAL IS (close to) 168, right? We're estimating.

4. A big question that you must face is: are you making the best, happiest use of your time?

5. The ultimate question: How many hours per week are you actually spending on anything you listed in question #1?

I am personally spending about 4 hours a day on long-term goals that I love. I spend the first hour working on a creative project which I also hope will make me money. I spend a half an hour working on my soul (at daily mass). I spend about 25-90 minutes a day exercising. And the last hour of my day is devoted to total relaxation.

6. How can you spend at least seven hours a week on something that you listed in #1?

Note

* "Multitasking" is a fictional concept invented in the 1990s to make people feel better about their lives, but there's only single-tasking with task-switching.

Costs of this fictional concept:

a) Multi-taskers are less happy; this is documented.

b) They feel hassled and overwhelmed.

c) They get less done.

d) Every time you switch jobs, they have "startup cost," which means it takes time to recover their concentration. Thus, not only do you get less done, you perform at a shallower level.

* A big question that you must answer is: are you making the *happiest* use of your time?

Why Are You Going to College?

Normal Reasons

Instructions: A) Check all that apply. B) Write a little.

The Point of This Assignment: If you know what you're trying to buy and/or experience, you're more likely to get it.

1. *Get a good job, and/or be an entrepreneur.*

Also known as "Return on Investment"; that is, you spend money on tuition in exchange for:

_____The Diploma

_____The Networking Connections

_____Other

Q. Are you going to college for practical, money-making reasons? If so or if not, please elaborate.

Q. How can you get the same set of skills outside of college?

Q. Think like a designer: What's the *second* way you could get the same skill set outside of college?

Q. Keep thinking like a designer: What's the *third* way you could get the same skill set outside of college?

2. ***Books and knowledge.*** Also called, the *liberal arts*. Perhaps 1 to 25% of the population these days goes to college to gather "useless' knowledge that makes you into a "well-rounded person." In the past, educated people thought we all needed to know quite a bit about math, science, literature, the arts, social studies like psychology and economics, business, and more. Without it, we'd be "technical barbarians"; we could fix machines but otherwise be crude and stupid. This is how *liberal arts*-minded people think.

In other words, people would be okay with paying $40,000 per year for four or five years to get a *liberal arts education*. If this sounds like what you desire, please check all that apply:

_____Read great books

_____Learn from great professors

_____Learn in-depth about the great issues (see the list above: math, science, literature, the arts, etc.)

_____Other

Q. What's missing from this line of thinking?

Q. Are you going to college for liberal arts reasons? If so or if not, please elaborate.

Q. How can you get the same set of skills outside of college?

Q. Think like a designer: What's the second way you could get the same skill set outside of college?

Q. Keep thinking like a designer: What's the *third* way you could get the same skill set outside of college?

3. Social reasons. Some people go to college to:

_____Have fun: enjoy the social life.

_____Join a fraternity or sorority.

_____Get married. After all, where else are you going to meet 500 to 10,000 people your age who perhaps share your worldview and hope to have substantial careers?

_____Other

Q. Are you going to college for social reasons? If so or if not, please elaborate.

Q. How can you get the same things outside of college?

Q. Think like a designer: What's the second way you could get these things outside of college?

Q. Keep thinking like a designer: What's the *third* way you could get these things outside of college?

Q. Some people go to college for social reasons. They succeed and have a great time. Then they flunk out of college. Discuss.

4. IDK yet. Some people don't know why they are going to college.

_____Every adult says it's the next step of life, and I (mostly) believe them.

_____My parents want me to go to college, so I'm going.

_____Honestly, I don't care too much about thinking about college. I'll worry about college—and the money to pay for it—during the summer after my senior year.

_____I am in denial. I am secretly freaking out and desperately worried, but I do my best to never think about it. If I pretend nothing is happening, then I will have a great life. Does anyone have any candy?

_____Other

Q. What is your first question about college?

Q. Second question?

Q. Third, fourth, and fifth questions?

5. I am going to college...

_____...for reasons not listed above.

Q. What are your reasons?

Q. How can you get the same things outside of college?

Windfalls and Monsoons

What Would You Do?

Scenario #1: Shortfall

Brenda is a college freshman at Benedictine, where she is committed to graduating with no debt because she doesn't want to work at any job she dislikes from ages 23 to 29. In high school, she worked one, two, and even three jobs simultaneously from time to time; she studied hard and earned 3.7 g.p.a.; she has a scholarship and her parents give her $5,000 per year.

Then tragedy strikes. Her Mom has a health problem and won't be able to work for the next two years. The family is in a bind. No vacation; no new car; smaller mortgage payments. And Brenda loses her $6,000 from her parents.

$5,000 over four years is $20,000, of course. But Brenda doesn't want $20,000 in student loan debt.

Help her make decisions. Here is her monthly budget:

Income

$400 Current Campus Job

$500 From savings

$500 From parents

$1,400 Total Income

Expenses

$817 Dorm & Meal Plan

$100 College Books

$40 Food

$100 Car (Gas, etc.)

40 Phone

100 Fun

25 Makeup, Hair

30 Dating

25 Clothes:

25 Christmas & Gifts

40 Tithe

58 Life Happens

$1,400 Total Expenses

Questions

1. Brenda needs an extra $500 that her parents can no longer give; her income is now $900, not $1,400. Should she cut $500 worth of items? What should she cut and/or replace?

2. Or maybe Brenda could make extra money per month. Keep in mind that her courses are difficult; she is taking 15 credit hours and studying 30 hours per week; that's 45 hours per week on school. She is also working 10 hours a week on campus. And she sleeps 7 hours a night (49 hours), and spends 2 hours per day on the basics of life (eating, dressing, commuting, exercising, etc.) Her social life right now is okay, but nothing spectacular. *So, should Brenda work extra? Doing what? How much could she make?*

2b. If you opt for Brenda to take on an additional job, how will you ensure that she keeps her scholarship, which essentially gives her $2,000 per month off tuition? Keep in mind how she is already spending 45 + 10 + 49 + 14 of her hours (see above) out of her 168-hour week.

3. Brenda could sell some of her possessions. Assume she doesn't have anything extreme. Maybe she has an old car; clothes; typical stuff for an 18 year old. What could she sell? And make how much?

4. Really get creative, now. How else could Brenda solve her problem?

Scenario #2: Blessing or Trap?

Andrew is also a college freshman at Benedictine. Similarly, he hopes to graduate with no debt. He feels lucky and blessed; his parents are paying for school—although he did cut their bill down by 60% due to various scholarships. If he doesn't maintain a 3.5 g.p.a., however, he loses it all.

One day, he receives a stunning job offer for an 18 year old. A local farmer within the city offers to pay Andrew an amazing $15 per hour! He must work 15 hours per week every week (with holiday weeks off). Essentially, that comes to $900 per month, or $8,100 during the school year. Summers are even better: Andrew can work 40 hours per week for eight weeks, and pocket an additional cool $4,800.

Right now, Andrew projects that he will graduate at the age of 22 and be dead broke. He'll have no debt, and perhaps zero to $500 in savings.

But at $8,100 + $4,800, Andrew can make $12,900 next year, and $52,600 after four years of college. Andrew can graduate with an extra $52,600. Even if taxes take away 33.3%, he can still pocket $35,067. Not to compare too much, but his friends will have debts ranging from $20,000 to $250,000. Some of them are majoring in fields with almost zero job prospects. They'll be working from 7 a.m. to 8 p.m. every day at two jobs with no social life just to survive. Andrew, on the other hand, could spend an entire year doing anything: backpacking through Europe and Asia; doing charity work anywhere; or even working to learn.

But Andrew does have concerns. He essentially spends 50 hours a week in class or studying. He sleeps 50 hours a week. He exercises 7. He needs 14 just for laundry, commuting, etc. And a guy's gotta have a social life.

Further, while the farming job looks fun and challenging, and would be a refreshing break from everything else he does, it doesn't necessarily fit with his career plans. Maybe it does (or maybe it doesn't). Can you see a link between engineering and farming?

Andrew is worried that if he takes this job, he may be too busy, have no outside life, and be distracting himself from what matters most to him: engineering.

1. What should Andrew do?

Most people will say "take it" or "don't take it." But it might be smarter to ask Andrew about five questions first before having an opinion. What are five excellent questions to ask Andrew?

2. Is there anyway Andrew can keep his options open?

Scenario #3: The Curse of Money

Your favorite cousin, who goes by the name Ty Rex Ninety X, has a song on YouTube that gets 20,000,000 views, and he gets picked up as a recording artist, and receives a $10,000,000 contract.

Swept up in this whirlwind, he goes on tour for two years, and occasionally sends you a text and every six months gives you a call. After all, you are childhood best friends. But he's super-busy, now.

Before he disappears for two years into the stratosphere, working/rocking hard, he gives you $100,000 after taxes. Unfortunately, he also posts on three social media sites that he did so. (The way that he did it was awesome, and the story itself gets 3,000 likes.) So, although you don't get pestered by strangers, most people around you know he gave you $100,000 after taxes.

1. What do you do with the $100,000?

2. Abruptly, you remember your other cousin, Allan, who received $101,000 when his great-grandfather passed away. Allan, at age 16, bought a sports car, went to Hawaii for two weeks, got all new clothes, and a ton of scuba gear. By the time he was 19, all he had left was $8.02 and a wrecked car.

Given the example of Allan, now what do you do with the $100,000?

3. But life is loaded with either emergencies (expensive) or chances to go wild. What safety controls will you put in place to keep yourself from accidentally blowing all the money?

4. You vaguely recall reading that psychologists and financial planners alike have studied this question, and found out that most people who get suddenly wealthy are actually far less happy a year later, and that pretty soon, all of the money is gone.

A minority, however, *grows* the money and is *more happy* a year later.

You decide you'd be a fool to ignore these 5,000 case studies, so you write a plan to grow the money and be happier. Write your plan now.

Scenario #4: Would You Give Up the Worst Thing That Ever Happened to You?

Samantha was attending Marquette University and loving it. But with tuition being $28,000 per year and living expenses about $12,000, she is spending $40,000 per year. That was great because with scholarships, parents, her savings from work, and other such things, everything was paid for. She would graduate in four years with her dream major.

But Samantha can't go to MU anymore. The reasons aren't known to us. Maybe her parents can't help. Maybe MU had to cut scholarships. Maybe she needs to live closer to home, in Kansas City.

But what we do know is that now she only has $1,000 per month--$12,000 per year—to operate with. Which means she can either graduate with $112,000 to $140,000 in student loan debt and an English major, or she can do something else with her life.

What else can she do? Raise income? Cut expenses? Sell things? Get creative? Lead a very different life? Dump her English major and become a chemist, which she has talent for, but hates?

1. Think of someone you know who is like Samantha: on one path, and then abruptly has to be on another. How can Samantha land on her feet?

2. Sometimes, the *worst thing that ever happens to a person* is—shockingly—the best thing. Arnold Schwarzenegger's father thought weightlifting was pointless—but Schwarzenegger became #1, and parlayed the work that went into being #1 into: volunteer work, acting, owning property, running restaurants, politics, and more. He developed a passion for knowledge, speaks six languages, and has led an incredible life.

A student may hate a really hard course with a difficult teacher—but maybe that class teaches them to work harder than anyone else.

An athlete might not like her coach—but maybe that helps her to develop the ultimate competitive edge.

In what way could Samantha turn this *crisis* into an *opportunity?*

Your Life's Personal Mission

Seven Questions

1. Please write anywhere from a paragraph to ten pages explaining what your Personal Mission (PM) is. A Personal Mission is *why you are on this earth*. For example, Mother Teresa decided to see the face of God in every neglected person. Thomas Edison decided to become an inventor, and he had 1,093 patents. Without accepting any interruptions, Arnold Schwarzenegger lifted weights five hours per day for six days every week so he could become the #1 bodybuilder in the world. Others decide their PM is to heal people.

Your (PM) can be short, long, a bullet point list, or in any format that works best for you. *You should be able to keep it with you every day, perhaps as the backdrop to your phone or laptop.*

2. Stuck? Ask adults who knew you when you were 0-12 years old what kind of kid you were. What were your hobbies? Who did you love? If you had a whole day just to play, what did you tend to do?

3. List 3 to 10 jobs or careers that fall within your Personal Mission.

4. List 3 to 10 jobs or careers that do *not* fall within your Personal Mission.

5. The more you write, the better. You can then whittle it down to the essentials.

6. What if you *didn't do a single thing* that did not fit your Personal Mission-- *for the rest of your life?* List 5 things that you would *stop doing right now* if you could because they don't fit it.

7. A Personal Mission is bigger than your career. Chances are, it also addresses your spiritual life, relationships, health, fun activities, and your entire existence.

Note: I honestly believe: if you do questions #1 & #2 above, you already know what your PM is—or you're close enough to get started without waiting for next week or next year. When some people say they don't know, it's often fear that's keeping them from saying. Maybe they think it isn't impressive enough. But if they do this exercise, they will experience a Moment of Clarity that may last for decades.

Disclaimer

This book is designed to provide accurate and authoritative information with regard to the subject matter covered. This information is given with the understanding that neither the author, related persons, or related companies is engaged in rendering legal, professional advice. Because the details of your situation are fact dependent, you should seek the advice of a competent professional.

Extended Table of Contents

APPENDIX: 19 EXERCISES